WITH GRATITUDE

Letters from a Psychiatrist

Dr. Suhaila A. AlShaali

With Gratitude
Copyright © 2025 Dr. Suhaila A. AlShaali
First published in 2025

Print: 978-1-76124-250-2
E-book: 978-1-76124-251-9
Hardback: 978-1-76124-252-6
UAE MEDIA: MC-02-01-9710127
Date:13th October 2025

All rights reserved. No part of this book may be reproduced, stored in a retrieval system, or transmitted by any means (electronic, mechanical, photocopying, recording, or otherwise) without written permission from the author.

Because of the dynamic nature of the Internet, any web addresses or links contained in this book may have changed since publication and may no longer be valid. The information in this book is based on the author's experiences and opinions. The views expressed in this book are solely those of the author and do not necessarily reflect the views of the publisher; the publisher hereby disclaims any responsibility for them.

The author of this book does not dispense any form of medical, legal, financial, or technical advice either directly or indirectly. The intent of the author is solely to provide information of a general nature to help you in your quest for personal development and growth. In the event you use any of the information in this book, the author and the publisher assume no responsibility for your actions. If any form of expert assistance is required, the services of a competent professional should be sought.

Publishing information
Publishing and design facilitated by
Passionpreneur Publishing
A division of Passionpreneur
Organization Pty Ltd
ABN: 48640637529

Melbourne, VIC | Australia
www.passionpreneurpublishing.com

CONTENTS

Dedication	v
Introduction	1
Chapter 1: From Dream to Reality	5
Chapter 2: Invisible Illness	15
Chapter 3: Mood Disorders	25
Chapter 4: Psychotic Disorders	41
Chapter 5: Domestic Abuse	55
Chapter 6: Neglect	73
Chapter 7: Maternal Mental Health	89
Chapter 8: Men's Mental Health	107
Chapter 9: Anxiety Disorders	123
Chapter 10: Substance Use Disorders	137
Chapter 11: Suicide	153
Chapter 12: Mental Disorders in the Healthcare Field	169
Conclusion	189
Acknowledgements	193
Author Bio	195

DEDICATION

*To all my patients, thank you for all the lessons
you've taught me and continue to teach me.*

INTRODUCTION

> *"I looked forward to speaking the language of medicine and trying to make basic treatment decisions. Above all, I hoped to experience human drama and emotion as it unfolded. There were the real-life anchors of medicine to my mind."* [1]

Dear reader,

What you're about to read is akin to a true story with some modifications, so that the people mentioned in this book remain unknown. While these stories are altered in one way or another, the sentiment of the impression remains what it genuinely was like for me. To give you some context, I'm a psychiatrist who happens to encounter a lot of ignorance when it comes to mental health. It's part of my daily life to debunk the myths and false perceptions that people have about mental wellness, but it's another challenge entirely to prove the existence of mental illness while advocating for it as a true illness.

The negative perception of mental illness is understandable. Whenever mental health comes up in social media, it's more influential from the viewpoint of the person suffering from mental health issues. You could recall the iconic scene of electroconvulsive therapy in *A Beautiful Mind* and find masses of ways to call psychiatrists evil. You can find a handful of popular television shows where mental healthcare professionals "act like they have no soul" or "drug people just to keep them sedated and make sure they're not a threat". It's understandable, because the vast and quickly changing discipline of psychiatry has portrayed its own trajectory as quite unstable. The inability to agree on standardized ways of testing, the multitude of opposing theories, the cultural discrepancies that can negate diagnoses…we can't agree with each other, so it's no wonder other specialties can't agree with us. However, I hope that reading other people's stories through my letters will reduce

Introduction

the skepticism towards psychiatry and those who struggle with mental illness.

As a disclaimer, I should warn you that the topics discussed in this book might be triggering. However, I request you to read with intention, to contemplate on those letters. You can open any page in the book and start reading. This book is written to show what is real and sometimes ignored. This is not a self-help or therapy book, rather it contains real stories along with real diagnoses.

All that aside, I never thought that I would be writing something like this. But something I read in one of my favorite memoirs reminded me that memories are ephemeral…so if they keep getting distorted with time, writing is a good way to immortalize them.[2] Since then, I've been journaling as much as I can so as to avoid losing those memories. At first, I didn't know why I was doing it. But eventually, I realized that I was writing what I didn't say my patients. I was inherently writing a letter to each patient I saw when they tugged at my heartstrings. One day it hit me – I thought I was writing to heal myself from the heaviness of what I witnessed, but I was actually writing in the hopes that something I said would resonate with someone. A part of me wishes that this book would show healthcare providers the impact and magnitude of mental illness. And the biggest part of me writing these letters is to let the sad souls know that they are not alone.

With gratitude,
Dr. Suhaila

References

1. Young, A. (2007). *What patients taught me: A medical student's journey.* Sasquatch Books.
2. Blythe, D.R. (2016). *Dark days: A memoir.* Da Capo Press.

Chapter 1

FROM DREAM TO REALITY

Life takes us in the most unusual directions towards discovering ourselves.

I was the youngest of five for a while. Sometimes I felt like a lonely child, so I was keen to fit in with my older siblings – especially when it came to playing games.

A Nintendo has slots for only four controllers, and I was the fifth. While my older siblings would be playing, they pretended that I was part of the action happening on screen. I discovered this soon enough, and even though I was not playing the game with them, I was still there in the midst of the laughter and fun. At times I'd watch them, and at other times I'd marvel at the titles in the bookcase around the television set. Those neatly arranged books, with beautiful bindings and covers, intrigued me. Most of these belonged to my mother, who has a background in psychology and sociology. I was far too young to delve into that world, but I was still curious. When she noticed that I was browsing through her books, my mother – bless her soul – started buying me sets of children's books. Another person who set me off on the journey of reading was my eldest sister; I used to watch her read on our way to school and admired her for this beautiful habit. Thus began my love for reading. What seemed like a lonely childhood became less isolating in that books became my friends; I formed closer bonds with my sisters and made friends through our shared reading interests.

Whenever my parents would take us to the mall, we spent as much time in bookstores as we did in toy stores. My mother tells a story about my childhood, wherein I would line up my toys and read to them or try to teach them.

In my adolescent years, I remember following in the footsteps of my sister when she was reading *Chicken Soup for the Soul*. The following two books set me on my journey to reading self-enhancement books: *Chicken Soup for the Teenage Soul* and *The 7 Habits of Highly Effective Teens*. I learned the phrase "paradigm shift", and that's what happened with me. I discovered the true power of these books to help me learn how to form connections with others. I started to think about various human traits like empathy, looking outside of yourself, and noticing other people's pain.

In the summer before my senior year of high school, I decided to buy a formal textbook of psychology and teach it to myself. That final year of school is when we finally shifted our focus in biology, and started learning human biology. I found myself enjoying that subject more than anything. Given my curiosity towards human behavior, I realized that the intersection of human biology and psychology was psychiatry. I must've been around 15 years old at that time, and had already decided I wanted to be a psychiatrist. I had a creative instinct for writing, and learning the ins and outs of human behavior made me a better writer. I still recall an essay I wrote for my

English class about the major themes in *Macbeth*, and how they related to Maslow's Hierarchy of Needs. My teacher told me that I had analyzed it beautifully.

My fascination towards the mysteries of the mind and what made people behave in certain ways seeped into every aspect of my life. Just as I was able to take a fictional story and analyze it, I started noticing people around me and thinking about their troubles from a psychoanalytic point of view. I may not have had the terminology or a complete understanding of why humans act as they do, but there was a seed of curiosity I was excited to nurture.

With my new understanding of empathy, I found myself wishing I could protect the people I met from the pain of their struggles. I found out that psychology and psychiatry are different, and that I would have to go through medical school and then specialize in psychiatry.

Psychology focuses on mental health in terms of how we feel, think and behave. Psychiatry focuses on the disordered ways we think, feel and behave. A psychiatrist's work has to do with diagnosing mental illness and using medication to manage it whereas a psychologist can help with diagnosis, but they focus on psychotherapies or talk therapy for management. I was hesitant about applying to study medicine initially, but I asked one of my teachers during a career fair what he thought about it. He responded with something I never forgot, something along the lines of:

*If you feel you have an ability to do something,
then you have a moral obligation to try.*

That day, I decided to pick up an application for the College of Medicine. I knew that I had to pursue my dreams and train to become a psychiatrist. Many young people enter medical school to become doctors, not knowing what they want to specialize in afterwards, or changing their mind along the way after their clinical experiences. This wasn't the case for me; I consider myself lucky in that I always knew that I'd be applying to specialize in psychiatry after graduating medical school. I was even luckier that my clinical experiences with psychiatry as a medical student only solidified my interest in this field. I can now say it was a dream I've had for half my life, and I'm grateful to have achieved it 15 years later. It was the hardest endeavor, and it took patience, grit, and a refusal to settle for anything less.

It was difficult to sacrifice parts of my social life. While other people my age were engaging in social activities, I was missing out because I always had so much studying to do. My weekly load of work and study was taxing. My final exams were more stressful, as they accounted for 90% of my grades (unlike other specialties that consider assignments, quizzes, midterms, and final exams for grading). Other than written exams, I had anxiety-inducing practical exams. These hardships continued after university. Training to become a psychiatrist didn't allow me to have a normal social life, as I was never in control of my working hours. I often worked on the weekend or during holidays, missing family gatherings, birthdays, and other important events. Since it was a training job, I had to study and take exams to become certified. I firmly believed it made sense to have to work this hard, because someday people would trust me with their wellbeing.

Thinking back to where it all started, the strong urge I have to help people enabled me to persevere despite challenges and failures. I'm inspired by my curiosity as well as an interaction I had early in my university years. A close friend was told by her university advisor that she may have depression and would benefit from seeking professional help. She confided in me about her struggle before she had informed her own family. She came from a conservative and religious family who viewed mental illness as a lack of faith, so she was afraid of telling her parents. She never ended up receiving help from a mental health professional. It broke my heart that this kindred soul was suffering in silence because of stigma. To this day, she goes through depressive episodes and relies on her friends for support. This kind of situation is all too common. Though this frustrates me, it also fills me with determination. It not only drives me when treating my patients, but also instilled in me a deep desire to spread awareness around mental illness in the community and attempt to dispel the shame and stigma associated with it.

When you see different things, you see things differently. Having been a resident of a country that provided me with the opportunity to encounter a multicultural population has been an impactful and insightful experience. I've seen patients who were crisis immigrants, patients who speak languages that I'd never heard of, patients who come from minority religious backgrounds.

And so, I've had a whirlwind journey through psychiatry. The one universal thing I've learned, though, is the importance of communication. By that, I mean the ability to speak the patient's language in two ways. The first is in a literal sense, when language barriers exist and you have to communicate through an interpreter... things can easily get lost in translation, potentially affecting a patient's outcome. The second is in the metaphorical sense, as in to find a way to relay the information to your patients in a way they're most likely to accept, aligned with their personal beliefs. These challenges (and many more) are learning opportunities enriching the way I view society, teaching me how to help people from different backgrounds, and allowing me to grow in the incredible field that is psychiatry.

Despite enjoying my daily practice of a doctor specializing in psychiatry, a part of me felt that I wanted to understand more than the medical aspect of human behavior. To realize this goal,

I embarked upon a journey to get my master's degree in the Psychology and Neuroscience of Mental Health. I didn't want to be the kind of psychiatrist who believes mental illness is entirely due to biological changes; instead, I wanted to understand mental health's psychological and social underpinnings. That's what made getting a master's degree alluring to me.

In the following chapters, I'm going to tell you about a few of the many people who have impacted me and taught me valuable lessons. I hope you'll read the letters I wrote to them and take them to heart.

CHAPTER 2

INVISIBLE ILLNESS

WHY SHOULD WE TALK ABOUT MENTAL HEALTH?

Wherever you go, you'll always live inside your mind.

In other words, you can't get away from your inner self, as much as you try to dismiss it. There's a reason we preach that there's no health without mental health. I came to realize this when I moved away from home to pursue my training in psychiatry. I always thought that once I finally got accepted to my training program of choice, I would stop worrying. Needless to say, that was not the case. My worry manifested as abdominal pain and I was getting ill more often. This prompted me to pay attention to my own mental wellbeing and how it was affecting my physical health. I would achieve a goal, then worry about the next goal I was chasing. Whether I lived in Ajman or Abu Dhabi, there was no running away from the worry of "the next step". Though the importance of mental wellbeing is becoming more recognized with time, there's still much work to be done in terms of awareness, education, and support for those suffering and those supporting them. As studies show, stigma towards mental illness is a worldwide phenomenon, even though there are cultural differences when it comes to how this stigma manifests.[1]

In this chapter, I'll briefly touch on the history of mental illness and how it's evolving. There are statistics regarding how common mental illness is and the devastating outcomes it could lead to – one out of eight people worldwide suffer from mental illness, as estimated by the WHO in 2019.[2] It's the duty of a psychiatrist to enlighten people and challenge their misconceptions. Mental wellbeing can no longer take a backseat in a world full of stressors and risk factors for developing illness. Hopefully, by the time you reach the end of this chapter, you'll have a better understanding of the overarching impact of mental illness.

THE INVISIBLE ILLNESS

So, what do we mean when we talk about mental illness being invisible? Many of those with a mental illness often don't have the telltale physical signs, which means that the mental struggles of many are unknown to others unless they decide to share that struggle.

This makes it quite likely that you or someone you encounter has experienced some form of mental illness. Whether in childhood or adulthood, all of us could have had an encounter with someone mentally struggling. Perhaps you didn't know the extent of their issues, but you did notice them behaving differently. Reflect on your reaction:

- Did you view them negatively?
- Did you feel uncomfortable communicating with them?
- Did you turn away and ignore them?

If your thoughts, reactions, and behaviors follow the aforementioned questions, then I urge you to rethink your beliefs about human behavior and mental health.

People have varying levels of transparency around their physical or mental health, but they're more likely to be open about physical health issues as these are generally deemed acceptable. Telling others "I have a doctor's appointment" doesn't have a negative connotation, whereas saying "I have a therapist appointment" still seems taboo. People who seek professional mental healthcare are viewed as less capable and are often encouraged to leave that aspect of their life unspoken as though it's a shameful issue.

Due to this stigma, there are many ways that people attempt to conceal having a mental illness. Professionally, I see this in the way people attending my clinic might cover their face with big sunglasses and a face mask so they're not recognized. Socially, I notice that if people are open about taking psychiatric medications, they refer to them as "medication for my nerves" to avoid using the word "psychiatry".

However, despite some pockets of bias, there's increasing awareness about mental health issues, with more people beginning to talk about them without hesitation.

※

A History of Stigmatization

What has changed about the way we used to treat those suffering from mental illness and the way we do now?

From around 1800, the Age of Enlightenment brought about the recognition of psychiatry as a medical specialty. However, care for those diagnosed with a psychiatric disorder was provided in asylums, geographically separated from hospitals and wider society. The rationale for asylums started off with good intentions. Institutionalizing patients was meant to provide them with adequate living conditions and care during a time of rapid urbanization, when they often couldn't be cared for by their families. However, those with mental illness were seen as unfit to be integrated in society and sequestered away in asylums, creating stigma.

By the 1950s, more patients worldwide lived in asylums than at any other time. This situation eventually caused more harm than good. As asylums were steadily overcrowded, they became associated with poor living conditions, bad hygiene, and ill-treated patients.[3]

In the United States, the Civil Rights Movement between 1954 and 1968 highlighted the cruelty of asylums. In the same period, new antipsychotic drugs gave rise to the idea that those with mental illness can live in society with the hope that new antipsychotics provided for a cure. Laws to preserve liberty meant that the mentally ill patients could not be institutionalized against their will. This was a game-changer. In 1963, the Community Mental Health Construction Act was passed, allowing for the creation of centers that provided mental healthcare in the community. Things continued to change in the US, as funding for mental healthcare became shared between states and the federal government. This caused the community mental healthcare facilities to close, and care for the mentally ill was integrated into community hospitals.[4] This process, which came to be known as de-institutionalization, was said to represent a long-awaited shift in the way care is provided. It was observed in North America, Europe and Australia, whereas it varied in the rest of the world.[5] Nowadays, we're witnessing a cultural shift where people are more likely to speak up about mental illness than people in the 1960s were.

The Changing Landscape of Mental Health

We can see similar changes happening all around the world. In the United Arab Emirates, for example, we're observing a situation wherein some hospitals have separate buildings for mental health patients, while others integrate psychiatry within the main hospital, as well as dedicating an entire separate hospital to mental illness. What makes this book important is that it highlights some defining mental health issues in our rapidly evolving society. We need to be more open and accepting of how this is a growing area of concern, because we're facing complex situations that create inner chaos, with this inner turmoil showing up in our behaviors and disrupting our mental wellbeing.

You can expect stories about different facets of mental health issues from this book, such as:

- mood disorders: types of depression, how they manifest, and the role of social support in recovery
- psychotic disorders: defining disorders like schizophrenia and addressing misconceptions about these disorders
- forms of abuse: violence, neglect, people vulnerable to abuse and the complexity of intervening in such situations
- maternal mental health: mental disorders occurring in the context of pregnancy in addition to the importance of mental support
- men's mental health: expectations that make men vulnerable and limitations to seeking help
- anxiety disorders: how anxiety manifests physically, as well as some common coping mechanisms (both healthy and unhealthy)
- substance use disorders: how common substance use disorder is, and misconceptions about those suffering with it
- mental illness in the healthcare field: perceptions of healthcare workers with mental illness and specialties at high risk

- suicide: risk factors, perception of life-taking, proposed underlying theories, and common misconceptions.

I'll dispel some of the myths surrounding these disorders. To become more enlightened and knowledgeable, it's vital that you recognize what's going on in the world around us when it comes to mental wellbeing. Like I said, no matter where you go, you'll always live inside your mind – so you might as well make it a healthy place to exist.

If there's one thing I hope you take away from this chapter, it's that mental disorder – though invisible – pervades all areas of our lives. We'll delve into the deeper aspects of mental health in the next chapters.

REFERENCES

1. Seeman, N. *et al.* (2016). 'World survey of mental illness stigma', *Journal of Affective Disorders*, 190, pp. 115–121. doi:10.1016/j.jad.2015.10.011.
2. *Mental disorders* (2022). *World Health Organization*. Available at: https://www.who.

int/news-room/fact-sheets/detail/mental-disorders (Accessed: 24 November 2024).
3. Fakhoury, W. and Priebe, S. (2007). 'Deinstitutionalization and reinstitutionalization: Major changes in the provision of Mental Healthcare', *Psychiatry*, *6*(8), pp. 313–316. doi:10.1016/j.mppsy.2007.05.008.
4. Yohanna, D. (2013). 'Deinstitutionalization of people with mental illness: Causes and consequences', *AMA Journal of Ethics*, 15(10), pp. 886–891.
5. Fakhoury, W. and Priebe, S. (2007). 'Deinstitutionalization and reinstitutionalization: Major changes in the provision of Mental Healthcare', Psychiatry, *6*(8), pp. 313–316. doi:10.1016/j.mppsy.2007.05.008.

CHAPTER 3

MOOD DISORDERS

WHEN EMOTIONS GO HAYWIRE

Worldwide, 280 million people are estimated to have depression.[1] The causes, however, aren't clear-cut. It was previously thought that a shortage of a certain hormone called serotonin was implicated; this is known as the monoamine or serotonin theory, which has been around for over 30 years.[2] However, advances in psychiatry have led us to understand this as only one part of a far bigger story.

In 2022, prominent British psychiatrist Dr Joanna Moncrieff published a notable study reviewing the evidence for the serotonin theory. Even though professionals continue to push this theory, there are negative outcomes in doing so. Most importantly as Dr Moncrieff notes, believing this theory affects how those with depression view their illness, putting them at risk of believing they're helpless in regulating their mood.[3]

Think of it this way. If you believed your illness was purely a chemical imbalance, it lends you to believing you need medications to recover, and you'd be skeptical about other methods that could lead to recovery. Though I'm not dismissing the importance of medications, I'm explaining this to provide hope for those struggling with depression and give them back a sense of agency.

Here's a patient who demonstrates the textbook symptoms of depression.

Dear Meera,

You were one of the quietest, most soft-spoken patients I've met. Your siblings brought you to the hospital from your hometown two hours away. You were nearly mute, only crying and mumbling sometimes. Your depression was so severe, you were almost catatonic. You needed help with everything like walking, getting up, getting dressed, eating, and all the simple self-care acts that the rest of us do without thinking. The kind of depression you had manifested with strong beliefs about religion, death, and the afterlife. You barely talked – but when you did, you asked me if you were between death and the afterlife and if Judgement Day had come. You were terrified that you'd died.

Your sister was also a troubled young woman. She left your family to study abroad, admitting to being diagnosed with depression and taking medication. She talked to you in the same soft-spoken manner you had. She'd keep telling you that you were going to be okay. She cracked jokes and you reacted. The first time I saw you smile is when your sister was around. I couldn't help but think how much love was there. I was witnessing the support of family. I was witnessing family act like family. Even though your parents rarely visited, your sister was there every day. She brought out light in you that I didn't see when the rest of your family members would visit.

There was something strong binding you to your sister, both deep sadness and unconditional love.

With gratitude,
Dr. Suhaila

AFTERTHOUGHTS

We talk about mental illness from a biopsychosocial perspective, and this patient highlighted all those aspects for me. Biologically, I thought about her sister and the genetic predisposition that might be implicated in her illness. Psychologically, I wondered if her personality type made her more prone to being depressed. More significant to me was the social aspect. I didn't only think of the social conditions that contributed to her depression; I also thought about it in terms of her recovery. This patient's relationship with her sister is what helped her, as well as helping the treating team get through to her. It solidifies the concept that people with mental illness are more likely to recover if they have social support. Meera's trust in her sister gave her hope, and it gave me hope.

Is everybody who's sad, depressed?

It's crucial to note that sadness is not depression. In an age where these two words are used interchangeably, the difference between them should be recognized. Sadness is an emotion, and all emotions come and go. The persistence and intensity of sadness is what qualifies it as one of the symptoms of depression. Clinical depression also has types, classified in both manuals used by psychiatrists: the Diagnostic and Statistical Manual of Mental Disorders as well as the International Classification of Diseases. These manuals are important guideposts in the mental healthcare field, as they direct our decision-making when it comes to making a diagnosis.

If you think about the statistic shared at the beginning of this chapter, it becomes apparent that you've most likely encountered an individual going through a depressive episode. Perhaps you notice a loved one isolating themselves, or a colleague not performing as well as they used to... or perhaps you've been going through a rough time where you find it difficult to get out of bed and do the simplest daily tasks. Because most of the symptoms of depression are subjective, it falls under the category of an 'invisible illness'.

THE RISK FACTORS FOR DEPRESSION

Even though we've yet to zoom in on the specific causes of depression, we do know its risk factors, how it manifests, and some possible methods of treating it. What makes a person prone to having a mood disorder like depression? There are known risk factors, such as not having a significant other (i.e. being single or divorced), living in a rural area, losing a parent before the age of 11, experiencing the death of a spouse, or being unemployed.[4]

The following story highlights how any of the aforementioned risk factors could trigger a depressive episode:

Dear Sabrina,

When you first arrived at the hospital brought by your ex-colleagues, you wouldn't speak to anybody. All we knew is that you were a middle-aged German woman, who'd lost your job because you'd lost your husband recently and stopped going to work as an architect. Day by day, we'd try to get you to talk, but you wouldn't even lift your head or respond when your name was called. You stopped eating or drinking; my supervisors thought that the only way to get you out of that state was to use electroconvulsive therapy, and that was when you spoke up and vehemently refused. At some point, you refused to come to the meeting room to see your doctors. Sadly, everyone around me was losing patience.

I came to your room one day, thinking you might be willing to talk if there wasn't an entire team of doctors around you. I decided to speak your native language, which I was in no way fluent in, but I'd learned to introduce myself when I did a brief rotation in Dresden as a medical student. "Hello, my name is Dr. Suhaila. I'd like to speak to you, but I don't speak German well. Would you mind helping me out?" I said to you in German. You responded with a hint of a smile, then you spoke back to me and fixed my grammar. We then had a brief conversation in English, in which you told me how lost you felt. I explained to you how important it was that you cooperate with your doctors so that we wouldn't be forced to attempt electroconvulsive therapy, which wasn't barbaric, but would be our only option if we couldn't help you get better.

The next day, you attended the meeting room. Your nurse told the team that you agreed to see us when she told you "Dr. Suhaila will be there". As the days passed, you slowly started to open up, and you were more amenable to our treatment suggestions. I watched you go from someone sitting in a wheelchair almost mute, to someone who spoke about what little hope you had and eventually, someone who stood on her own two feet ready to face her life again. Before leaving the hospital, you thanked me, shook my hand, and said "Auf Wiedersehen".

With gratitude,
Dr. Suhaila

AFTERTHOUGHTS

This was the first time I had a patient who recognized me personally. I thought about one of my supervisors who mentioned speaking the patients' language, adopting that advice literally. Though it was a small gesture, I noticed how big of a difference it made in getting through to a patient, giving her a safe space to share her struggles, giving her power back, and getting her to consider accepting help. This patient who didn't want to be helped changed her mind when she felt heard. Her farewell to me was a realization that it's not only the patients who need us…as doctors, we need our patients to fulfill our mission as Allah entrusted us to.

EXPLAINING MOOD DISORDERS

Among the variety of mood disorders, depressive disorder and bipolar disorder are the ones we encounter most often. As I've mentioned, depressive disorder includes sadness as one of its criteria. It also includes the inability to feel joy from activities previously enjoyed, sleep issues, appetite changes, loss of energy and concentration, feelings of overwhelming guilt, slowness in movement, and thoughts of death. The severity of depression is classified based on how many of these symptoms patients experience. Further classification depends on the episodes, as patients might either go through one episode or experience recurrent ones.

Bipolar disorder occurs when a patient experiences depressive episodes (as explained above) alternating with manic episodes. Mania includes a feeling of elation or irritability, increased energy, sleep deficits, feelings of grandiosity, being talkative, having racing thoughts, experiencing an increase in activity, and being distractible and impulsive. These two types of episodes are imagined to be on opposite poles, hence the name. In between episodes, patients generally experience periods of normalcy. Even a single manic episode is enough for a diagnosis of bipolar disorder.

Here's a visualization of what these two mood disorders would seem like:

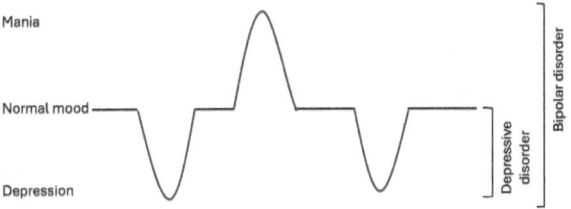

There are further modifiers for a diagnosis of depressive disorder or bipolar disorder, but those are outside the scope of this book. By now, you've gained some knowledge about these disorders; by reading the upcoming letters, you'll hopefully understand more about what they feel like.

As a trainee in psychiatry, the first time I interviewed a patient independently was an unforgettable interaction:

Dear Rashed,

"I'm going to throw this tissue box at you if you don't stop talking!" – This is what you said to me when I tried to interview you. It was early in my career, and you were the first patient I interviewed

in full-blown mania. The police brought you to the emergency department after you'd complained to them that your brothers were abusing you. You said they were jealous of you because you were the spoiled youngest sibling, your father's favorite, and because you knew you were better than them. You told me that they shaved your head because you kept dying it bright colors and they thought you were inappropriate. And as a traditional family, they were strict about cultural sensitivity and public perception. At that point, I had no way to know if anything you were saying was true.

You spoke so quickly, and so much. I found it almost impossible to redirect you. Your elated mood quickly turned into irritability, and you threatened to be hostile. Nevertheless, I stood my ground – accepting the challenge and telling myself that I couldn't let you faze me. Even though you presented a clear picture of bipolar disorder, my supervisor wanted me to keep interviewing you until I elicited your manic symptoms: talkative, grandiose, distractible, impulsive, with flights of ideas. I kept telling myself that this was a learning experience.

Later, we interviewed your father, who told us that you had indeed been abused by your siblings because they had no understanding of your illness and viewed your behavior as defiant. Dying your hair, constantly getting fined for speeding, never finishing your studies – these were symptoms of an illness that your brothers thought were character flaws and therefore wanted to teach you a lesson.

Due to the way the system is structured, I wasn't the one who got to follow up with your care, but I won't forget what you taught me.

With gratitude,
Dr. Suhaila

AFTERTHOUGHTS

When I reflect about the learning experience I gained from interviewing this patient, I recognize that I was learning to deal with an uncooperative patient and to understand my skills and limitations when it comes to interviewing someone in a manic episode. What stuck with me is that I was glad I didn't discredit what this patient was telling me simply because I could clearly tell he was going through an episode. If I'd decided to ignore him and squared away his accusations as delusions, I might have given him the wrong diagnosis. That day, I didn't only learn how to handle a tough interview…I also learned the importance of believing my patients.

Takeaways

The less we talk about mood disorders, the less likely it is that people living with them will seek help. You might wake up one day and be surprised by the news that somebody you know or used to know took their own life – and you would think to yourself if you'd ever noticed them suffering, or wondered what they were going through.

When it comes to depressive disorder, 65% of patients suffering will have thoughts of suicide and 10% of them will attempt to take their own life. It's incredibly sad to think that lives have been lost when their disorder could have been managed. Help is available, which I know to be true because I've seen people achieve recovery and remission. Recovering refers to getting out of an episode. Remission is a state where the disorder is still present, but the patient has achieved a state in which the symptoms haven't manifested for a period of time. Patients who utilize any forms of help available – whether it's talk therapy, medication, social support or a combination of these – are likely to recover and achieve a sense of normalcy. It's up to all of us as a society, and especially healthcare providers, to support those who suffer until they're able to regain their strength.

Though mood disorders usually tend to be chronic and thus can't be entirely cured, there are ways to empower those suffering in a way that teaches them to live a better life despite the chronicity of their disorder. One of the most impactful things I've heard a therapist say is:

> *Mental illness doesn't get better itself, but people get better at dealing with it.*
>
> —DR. JESSICA ANDERS

References

1. Institute of Health Metrics and Evaluation. Global Health Data Exchange (GHDx). https://vizhub.healthdata.org/gbd-results/ (Accessed 25 November 2024).
2. Heninger, G., Delgado, P. and Charney, D. (1996). 'The revised monoamine theory of depression: A modulatory role for monoamines, based on new findings from monoamine depletion experiments in humans', *Pharmacopsychiatry*, *29*(1), pp. 2–11. doi:10.1055/s-2007-979535.
3. Moncrieff, J. *et al* (2022). 'The serotonin theory of depression: A systematic umbrella review of the evidence', *Molecular psychiatry*, *28*(8), pp. 3242–3526.
4. Harrison, P.J. *et al.* (2018). *Shorter Oxford Textbook of Psychiatry*. Oxford: Oxford University Press.

Chapter 4

PSYCHOTIC DISORDERS

A DISTORTED REALITY

Imagine not being able to tell what's real and what's not.

Losing touch with reality is one way to describe psychosis, which could be a terrifying feeling for those who experience it. To understand what that's like, think back to a situation in which you had a completely different point of view than someone else, where you were entirely unable to believe or trust their perspective, yet couldn't seem to communicate that to them – that's a frustrating experience. In a way, psychosis is an extreme version of that.

Here's a story about a patient at the intersection between major depressive disorder and psychotic disorder.

Dear Marissa,

I keep wondering what happened to you to make you get to the point that you genuinely believed you deserved to suffer. You were not only severely depressed, but you also had nihilistic thoughts. You kept repeating that your soul was taken by Jesus and your body is left in this world to suffer for your sins. Your thoughts were delusional, but they somehow made sense to you. In the first few days of interviewing you, you kept repeating "I have no soul". You stopped eating because you believed you were a hollow body.

It gutted me to watch you cry every day; we needed to lift your mood. We needed you to let go of these delusions that made you unable to function. We had no choice but to start you on medication. Thankfully, you cooperated with our plan and didn't refuse to take your medication. Slowly, you started to improve and get closer to your baseline. When you started to speak more freely, we asked you where you thought your feelings of guilt were coming from. You replied, "I used my salary to go out with my friends instead of using it to support my family". It shocked me that guilt that arises from such a small incident led to existential guilt.

You got better eventually. Before you left the hospital, we asked you how you felt again and this time you said, "I now know I was ill, but I know that Jesus loves me because he brought me here where you could help me."

With gratitude,
Dr. Suhaila

Afterthoughts

Marissa's story taught me that faith plays a role in mental illness. When she was unwell, her delusions revolved around religion. When she was well, she felt stronger because of her faith. It taught me that we should encourage people to use faith as a protective factor when it works for them and as long as they express their wishes to do so. Religion is a protective factor while out-of-proportion religious guilt is harmful, so it's understandably a double-edged sword. Most importantly, I learned that the use of faith in recovery from mental illness isn't a black-or-white decision. To be clear, I'm not dismissing its positive effect. That being said, Marissa's experience made me open my mind.

Psychosis Explained

There are types of psychotic disorders which are sub-classified in the two manuals we use most frequently as psychiatrists. We already explained that psychosis refers to a distorted perception of reality. This manifests as delusions, illusions or hallucinations, and disorganized thinking or behavior.

Delusions are described as false beliefs that are held strongly despite evidence to the contrary, and they are not better explained by the individual's background in terms of culture and religion. For example, in a culture that follows religious teachings, believing in miracles is not classified as a delusion; however, if an individual believes they are a messenger of a deity, that would be a delusion. There are types of delusions, commonly paranoia or grandiosity. Illusions are misperceptions of existing stimuli. Hallucinations are misperceptions of non-existing stimuli involving the senses (auditory, visual, gustatory, olfactory, tactile).

Although psychosis is a general term for the cluster of symptoms described above, it's not a diagnosis in itself. Rather, it's a general term encompassing a raft of different disorders including schizophrenia, mania, depression, brain injury, delirium, and dementia, and others. Additionally, it can occur as an effect of medications or other substances.[1]

Here's a story about a man who suffered a psychotic episode after sustaining trauma to his head.

Dear Ahmad,

You came to the clinic for the first time with your cousin. You wanted him to speak for you, as you thought he was going to take you someplace else...to the neurology clinic.

Roughly three years back, you were in a road traffic accident in which you sustained a severe head injury and broken bones. Afterwards, you were described as "never quite the same". "In what ways has his behavior changed after the accident?" I asked your cousin. He replied "Ahmad is a highly educated officer with a degree in engineering. After the accident, his suspicions got the best of him. He was unable to work and was transferred to a desk job. He was showing no interest in anything except the idea that he is being followed. His relationship with his wife deteriorated as he became impulsive; they are now separated."

When I asked to speak to you alone, you asked "What do you want from me? All you doctors do is hurt me. The surgeon who operated on my brain was trying to kill me. Why else would he cause me this much pain?".

On review of your chart, I realized that you go to the pain clinic often but you don't accept pain medications. You insist that your arm was manipulated by the surgeon who treated your fracture in a way to continue causing you pain. You showed psychotic signs, and I wondered about your pain. Were you having a delusion that you were in pain? Were you experiencing phantom pain? Or was your pain purely physical? It was your cousin who brought you here, and you wanted to see a neurologist. You believed that you had an illness, but you didn't believe it was mental.

Sadly, you lost follow-up with mental health services and I never got to know how your condition turned out. I can only hope that you received some form of treatment or rehabilitation that is suited to your condition and that it reignited the light inside of you.

With gratitude,
Dr. Suhaila

Afterthoughts

Even though the explanation of psychosis seems simple in a textbook, I only understood its complexities when I met Ahmad. I struggled to think about how we could get him to accept help, so I imagined the thought process going on in his mind. This taught me that even though there are clear ways to describe psychiatric symptoms, our understanding of them widens when we think of the different causes of such symptoms. This also means that not every patient with the same cluster of symptoms requires the same management, so the causes are important to consider. I genuinely wished somebody like Ahmad would end up in a rehabilitation program.

Types of Psychotic Disorders

The majority of psychotic disorders I've encountered include brief psychotic disorder, schizophrenia, schizoaffective disorder, and delusional disorder. There are other causes of psychosis, which could be associated with depressive disorder, bipolar disorder, or dementia. Additionally, it could be secondary to another medical condition or an effect of a substance or medication.

Schizophrenia manifests with delusions, hallucinations, disorganized speech and behavior, diminished emotional expression, and loss of interest or motivation.[2] It's one of the chronic and most stigmatized mental disorders. I'd like you to be aware of the major misconceptions that contribute to stigma: a patient with schizophrenia is likely to be violent or dangerous, schizophrenia cannot be treated, patients with schizophrenia can infect others with their disorder, and patients with schizophrenia are lazy and can't function as others can.[3]

The claims mentioned above are unfounded as someone with a different reality than you can still live with some sense of normality. This mental disorder might mean that those who are living with the patient need to make adjustments to the aspects of their daily life. But to say that it cannot be treated contributes to negative outcomes. We need to change our expectations of those with schizophrenia, and this needs to be done by the treating team, the patients' families and loved ones, and society at large. We can start by giving hope to those with schizophrenia and empower them in their rehabilitation.

One of the therapeutic interventions in the community psychiatry department is providing activities for unemployed people with chronic mental disorders, which gives those patients a routine to help mitigate acute relapses.

Here's a story about a patient who offers a positive example of living with chronic schizophrenia while regularly attending the activity center.

Dear Ibrahim,

I met you on my first day in the community psychiatry department. You walked into my office sternly saying "Al-Salam Alaikom, are you new here?". You seemed serious. I told you I was new in this department. Your face immediately changed and you said, "I'm Ibrahim, everyone here knows me because I sing well." So I asked you what kind of music you like and you told me you love a certain Arab singer who happens to be one of my favorites. Then you asked if I had time to listen to you sing. You made my morning on that first day.

You're loved by all the staff in the community psychiatry department. You walk into all our offices twice a week never failing to say good morning to all of us. You have a childlike disposition, which makes sense – you're a middle-aged man who believes you're five years younger than your real age.

In the next few weeks, you visited my office every morning you attended the department for your rehabilitation and daily activities. It took you a while to remember my name, but once you got used to seeing me, you never forgot it.

On a particularly difficult day, you came into my office to strike a conversation, insisting on giving me the juice box you bought for yourself. You went on one of your typical monologues and I remember asking you how you always stay so happy. You answered, "I like to help people," and you told me about how you call the other patients that are signed up in the activity center to make sure they're attending. You come in regularly to help yourself, you help other patients, and you wanted to help me by offering me your juice, saying "in case you hadn't had breakfast today." What a pure soul you are.

With gratitude,
Dr. Suhaila

Afterthoughts

I started thinking about how kind and lovable Ibrahim is, and how frustrating it is when people assume somebody like him is violent. I wish anyone with the misconceptions mentioned would meet Ibrahim. He's calm, always well-dressed, and well-mannered with a kind heart. He reminded me to get outside of myself. Knowing that somebody like him – living with chronic schizophrenia – can derive happiness from helping others was a gentle reminder that I ought to be doing that too. This interaction truly humbled me.

Takeaways

I hope this chapter shed light on the reality of psychosis. If you understand how hard it is to lose touch with reality, you can empathize with those with psychotic disorders. We also need to be kinder and gentler towards their struggle. Remember that if we keep stigmatizing them, they're likely to experience negative outcomes like frequent relapses, ineffectiveness of rehabilitation, homelessness and even suicide.[4] When we describe these patients with words like "psycho" or "crazy" or imply that they should be locked up in a "mental hospital", we're creating a greater disconnect due to insensitivity and lack of empathy. I urge you to be careful with your words for that reason. And for healthcare workers, I urge you to look into the breadth and depth of these patients' symptoms to find out how to best help them. The tragedy of modern psychiatry is that we often fall into the pit of checking off categorical symptoms and end up neglecting the *meanings* of symptoms.

> *"All I can think is, it's not like the old days, when some stoical psychoanalyst would hear you out for hours and hours, withholding judgement while you lay on their sofa expelling your word-salad thoughts and florid delusions. Nowadays, it's about pharma, drugs, and it hardly matters that all those tangled thoughts originate from a sentient being – a real person."*[5]
>
> —MIRA T. LEE

REFERENCES

1. Ganti, L., Kaufman, M. S., & Blitzstein, S. M. (2016). *First Aid for the Psychiatry Clerkship, Fourth edition*. McGraw Hill Professional.
2. American Psychiatric Association. (2022). Schizophrenia spectrum and other psychotic disorders. In *Diagnostic and statistical manual of mental disorders* (5th ed., text rev.).
3. Dinan, T. G. (1999). Schizophrenia: illness, stigma and misconceptions. *Irish Journal of Psychological Medicine, 16*(1), 3–4.
4. Ibid.
5. Lee, M. T. (2019). *Everything Here Is Beautiful: A Novel*. Penguin.

Chapter 5

DOMESTIC ABUSE

THE FRIGHTENING RISK FOR THOSE WITH MENTAL DISORDERS

When you think of people with mental disorders, do you automatically associate them with violence?

The prejudice is prevalent and exaggerated, with most people believing in the idea that those with mental disorders are violent or abusive when in fact, studies show those with mental disorders are more likely to be victims of abuse than those without mental disorders,[1] which makes sense. When you think about the effects of having a mental disorder, the person becomes vulnerable or susceptible to being taken advantage of. For example, if a patient lives with a depressive disorder, they're likely to feel overbearing guilt. The people around this patient can use that guilt as a means of manipulation.

A systematic review and meta-analysis revealed that all pooled odds ratios estimated show that having a mental disorder as a woman increases the likelihood of being subjected to domestic violence by their partner when compared to women without mental disorders.[2] Another study showed that there's a link between the onset of abuse and the time of being diagnosed with mental disorder.[3]

Below is a story of how being diagnosed with depressive disorder can have a tragic outcome.

Dear Mariam,

When I first got the call for a consultation about you, I was told you had come to the emergency department after a minor fall and that you were complaining of insomnia. I arrived to find a pleasant, put-together lady. I introduced myself and asked how I can help. You spoke mostly about your trouble sleeping. The more I questioned you, the more you seemed anxious. I had to ask about your injuries and whether you were subjected to any sort of abuse; that's when you became silent and began to tear up. It's like you were wearing a mask to cover your sadness, and it suddenly fell off.

You opened up to me about how your husband had started beating you a year ago. About the same time you were diagnosed with depressive disorder, your husband started to act harshly towards you. He would blame you for the depressive symptoms when daily activities became difficult for you. He called you a bad wife and mother when you were going through depressive episodes. Rather than supporting you, he called you "insane". To add insult to injury, he also threatened to have your children taken away from you because he said he could get a report of your mental records to support his claim that you are an unfit mother. I wondered if you had asked the emergency physician for a report of your injuries and if you were planning to report the abuse. "No, please, I don't want to cause trouble...I didn't want anyone to find out," you said. I asked what keeps you strong; you replied: "I have 3 children, and I'd rather have him take his anger out on me than on them".

There was no way for me to change your social situation and keep you safe. I had to respect your wishes. It wasn't a situation I could manage with medications or by admitting you to the hospital. I asked again how I can help; you responded: "You did, you listened and your reminded me that my children keep me strong". I watched you leave the emergency department, feeling awe and despair at the same time. There you go, a bright young lady masking her struggles to keep her children safe...But I still see you in my mind from time to time, and I pray that you found safety.

With gratitude,
Dr. Suhaila

AFTERTHOUGHTS

Mariam's story was a harsh jolt of reality that left me conflicted. It had me thinking about our limitations as doctors when it comes to helping our patients. I wanted to ask the emergency physicians to write a report detailing the physical trauma that her husband had inflicted on her so she could use it to report him, but she didn't want to. She also refused my recommendation to start taking medications. I was bound by the principle of autonomy to accept and respect her decisions. While discussing her case with my supervising specialist and expressing my frustration that I felt like I did nothing to help, she told me "Sometimes helping a patient is just by listening to them and empowering them" – I'll always remember this, because it taught me that my role in improving my patients' lives might not always be the one I expect it to be.

WHAT IS DOMESTIC ABUSE AND WHY DON'T WE TALK ABOUT IT?

Domestic abuse or violence is an act or pattern of acts when one person's behavior is threatening, coercive, or abusive towards another person over the age of 16, occurring between spouses or family members. Types of abuse may be psychological, physical, sexual, financial and emotional.[4]

We avoid speaking openly about the problems inside a home, as it is considered to be socially and culturally unacceptable. Those with a mental disorder are already stigmatized, and being victims of abuse is an additional challenge. Research shows victims are less likely to disclose being abused if they felt emotional constraint, having no safe place to turn to, or being bound by finances and threats.[5]

There are different factors affecting the likelihood that a victim of abuse would be open about their experience. When it comes to social and legal ramifications of reporting abuse, some might believe that involving authorities is taboo, as it associates their family name with shame and disgrace, and they worry about how that would affect their status in society. There are also healthcare aspects to consider when a victim comes forth to report abuse. A study has shown that victims might be hesitant to disclose abuse to healthcare workers due to fear of consequences to their safety or due to the healthcare worker's negative attitude toward them.[6]

These barriers need to be broken down for us to move towards a safer society.

Here's a story about someone who's been subjected to violence by his family.

Dear Mohammed,

I found your story to be one of the most devastating I've encountered. A 19-year-old with eight siblings, living in poverty. I spoke to your father mainly because you wouldn't speak to me other than to say, "I want to go home". Your father told me about your diagnosis, that you had schizophrenia and an intellectual disability, and you were given medications that you're refusing to take. He complained that you were being difficult at home and hitting your siblings. Your father then asked, "Isn't there somewhere you can keep him for a few months until he's normal again?" – I then remembered that I know your story. I attended an ethics committee meeting wherein your case was discussed.

I tried to reason with your father to change his expectations of you, but your father started talking about how you are unbearable at home. He insisted for you to be admitted to the hospital. He told me you'd been hospitalized when you were still an adolescent in your home country and that your doctor was abusive and had hit you on the head.

When you couldn't speak to me to confirm it. I had to rely on my prior knowledge of your situation to make a decision about how to help you. "Psychiatrists need to be aware of this patient and that he has an abusive father" – one of the things that made me doubt your father's reliability. It's not fair that you live in an overcrowded accommodation which lends you to more abuse. It's not fair that your family is the one subjecting you to it, physically by beating you or chaining you, and psychologically by mistreating you. I am torn apart when I think about how all this abuse must have exacerbated your condition. And most heart-breaking is that you didn't have the voice to speak up for yourself, so we were going to have to do it for you.

With gratitude,
Dr. Suhaila

Afterthoughts

I'm not at liberty to say what happened to Mohammed after my interaction with him. I won't forget that he taught me the importance of giving my patients a chance to show me who they are, the benefit of the doubt and patience. Believing his father's words as a reliable historian would have been a mistake, so I tried to find Mohammed's voice through his behavior, by attempting to call his mother, and by looking at his previous medical records. I tried to go the extra mile and looked everywhere so that I could make the right decision. Eventually, I did what I could do to guarantee his safety, and I hoped that as his story moves along, his voice is always heard.

The devastating impact of domestic abuse

Domestic abuse is a worldwide phenomenon. It's not limited to developing countries, even though there's said to be a positive correlation between low socioeconomic status and abuse.[7,8] The UK

Department of Health released a statistic revealing that one out of every four women in England and Wales are subjected to domestic violence, in addition to one out of every six men.[9]

Domestic abuse ought to be a public health priority. Its consequences include injuries, chronic physical illness, poor overall health, negative perinatal effects, substance misuse, mental disorders, and even suicide.[10] Up to 60% of women with mental disorders go through domestic violence.[11]

Consider the impact on the health of a society when victims suffer without being able to seek solace. When someone grows up in a home environment that feels unsafe, anywhere else feels just as unsafe to them. If compounded by a mental disorder, this increases their susceptibility to becoming victims of abuse.

You're about to read a story about a woman whose diagnosis trajectory changed due to domestic abuse.

Dear Ilham,

You were heavily sedated, lying on the transport bed and not moving when the team brought you from the emergency department to the mental health unit. Your father and brothers were there to tell us that you had paranoid schizophrenia, that you believed your family was out to get you, so you stopped accepting the medications you were given to treat your schizophrenia. Your family explained that you have been acting irrationally, demanding things to be done at once when you ask and branching out of your family's values. They were suggestible when questioned about you, answering yes to all the symptoms we asked if you are displaying. But the way you ended up in the hospital today did not align with what your family said. They accused you of breaking things and attempting to beat them – but you were the one who had physical bruises.

The next day, you were more alert. You told us your story. That you had been married off at a very young age to an elderly man and that you developed obsessive compulsive disorder and then got divorced; that your family would keep telling you that this is "demonic possession" and attempt to take you to faith healers. You come from an extremely strict family that is hardwired to believe women are not meant to drive, study, work, and have freedom of choice. You said that you got into an altercation with your brother because he threatened to hit you after finding out you applied for a job in the mosque to teach Qur'an to children. You mentioned that because your OCD manifests as obsessions of cleanliness, you spend a lot of time washing yourself... and when this would happen, your family would abuse you and convince you that you are psychotic. Everything you said made logical sense. But it was difficult to decide which information to take into account when it comes to two conflicting stories.

Over the next few days of observing you in the inpatient unit, it was apparent that you did not show psychotic symptoms, but you did show OCD symptoms. And here, your family was trying to force onto you medications that are meant to treat schizophrenia. While discharging you from the hospital, I made sure to give you an appointment seven days after.

You ended up going to the clinic to see one of my senior physicians. After that physician saw you, he called me and said: "It's more likely that she has OCD than schizophrenia. We reached an agreement with her family". My heart felt some peace when I heard that you're receiving the help you need, the way you need it, and from one of the best doctors I know.

I'll rest a little better knowing that you're in safe hands.

With gratitude,
Dr. Suhaila

AFTERTHOUGHTS

When it comes to abuse, it's hard to stay hopeful when you feel helpless. But Ilham showed me the importance of believing what you see and not just what you hear, and that recovery is possible – especially when a correct diagnosis is made. Her diagnosis trajectory highlights just how important it is to observe and let our patients – just like any other human – show us who they really are. Wherever Ilham is now, I'd like to believe she's continuing her diploma, and teaching wherever she wants (while driving herself there, of course!). Some might say my belief is misguided, but I believe in hope – and I never stop hoping for Ilham.

Mental disorders don't discriminate. However, we often discriminate against those with mental disorders and discount their experiences with abuse. The similarity bias proposes that we're more likely to help people who have something in a common with us.[12] This is your reminder of how important it is to see those suffering as similar in order to humanize them. After all, it can happen to any of us. As our world continues to change, so should we. Empathy is an ingrained trait in us; it's our job to foster it in a way that supports victims of domestic abuse with or without a mental disorder.

Takeaways

I aim to tell these stories so that it will nudge you to rethink your view of those with mental disorders and their likelihood to become violent. I hope that now, "If you see something, you say something". You might not have the power to completely be sure that the abuse has stopped, but as this chapter suggests, even the minimal ways we help can make a difference.

For anyone you know who might be a victim of domestic violence, asking them directly could change their lives. And as healthcare providers, we need to ensure our patients are having a positive experience that leads to trust, directly asking the question about abuse (even though it seems daunting), and we need to make sure that the environment our patient is in feels safe to them. We must do whatever we can so that they no longer have to be on edge, wondering when the next act of abuse is coming.

> *"The abuser's most skillful trick is to make his abuse invisible."* [13]
>
> —JESS HILL

And it is our job to make it visible.

References

1. Stuart H. (2003). Violence and mental illness: an overview. *World psychiatry: Official journal of the World Psychiatric Association (WPA)*, *2*(2), 121–124.
2. Roberts, G. L., Williams, G. M., Lawrence, J. M., & Raphael, B. (1999). How Does Domestic Violence Affect Women's Mental Health? *Women & Health*, *28*(1), 117–129. doi:10.1300/j013v28n01_08
3. Khalifeh, H., Moran, P., Borschmann, R., Dean, K., Hart, C., Hogg, J., Osborn, D., Johnson, S., Howard, L. M. (2014). Domestic and sexual violence against patients with severe mental illness. *Psychological Medicine*, *45*(4), 875–886. doi:10.1017/s0033291714001962
4. Home Office. (2013). Definition of domestic violence and abuse: Guide for local areas. Home Office.
5. Francis, L., Loxton, D., & James, C. (2017). The culture of pretence: a hidden barrier to recognising, disclosing and ending domestic violence. *Journal of Clinical Nursing*, *26*(15–16), 2202–2214. doi:10.1111/jocn.13501
6. Heron, R. L., & Eisma, M. C. (2021). Barriers and facilitators of disclosing domestic violence

to the healthcare service: A systematic review of qualitative research. *Health & Social Care in the Community, 29*(3), 612–630. doi:10.1111/hsc.13282

7. Trickett, P. K., Aber, J. L., Carlson, V., & Cicchetti, D. (1991). Relationship of socioeconomic status to the etiology and developmental sequelae of physical child abuse. *Developmental Psychology, 27*(1), 148–158. doi:10.1037/0012-1649.27.1.148

8. Zielinski, D. S. (2009). Child maltreatment and adult socioeconomic well-being. *Child Abuse & Neglect, 33*(10), 666–678. doi:10.1016/j.chiabu.2009.09.001

9. Khalifeh, H., Moran, P., Borschmann, R., Dean, K., Hart, C., Hogg, J., …Howard, L. M. (2014). Domestic and sexual violence against patients with severe mental illness. *Psychological Medicine, 45*(4), 875–886. doi:10.1017/s0033291714001962

10. Ibid.

11. Heron, R. L., & Eisma, M. C. (2021). Barriers and facilitators of disclosing domestic violence to the healthcare service: a systematic review of qualitative research. *Health & Social Care in the Community, 29*(3), 612–630. doi:10.1111/hsc.13282 *The Relationship Between Domestic*

Violence and Mental Health. (2022, October 18). High Country Behavioral Health.
12. Cascio, E.V. and Martin, L. M. (2011) *House and psychology: Humanity is overrated.* Hoboken, N.J.: John Wiley.
13. Hill, J. (2020). *See what you made me do: power, control and domestic abuse.* Oxford University Press.

CHAPTER 6

NEGLECT

AN OVERLOOKED FORM OF ABUSE

When you think of your childhood, do you ever recall experiences in which you were denied your needs?

Neglect is the most common form of maltreatment in childhood.[1] Neglect might not be one of the first forms you think of when you think of abuse; this is because it's considered to be passive, whereas other forms of abuse – physical, sexual, or emotional/psychological – are seen as active.[2]

Below is a harrowing story of a neglected newborn.

Dear Malak,

I got to meet your mother, twin sister, and other siblings. I'm told you were an identical twin, so even though you weren't there in the room, I had a picture in my head of what you might have looked like.

At the age of 16, your mother was forced into a marriage and had multiple unplanned pregnancies. You were the last of those. Your mother was overwhelmed and frustrated with all the responsibilities forced upon her. Sadly, she felt like she needed to take it out on someone. You weren't the "quiet baby", you were the loud and difficult one...As a twin, your mother had polarizing thoughts of you and your twin – one of you was the "good twin" and one of you was the "bad twin". Your mother admitted to leaving you to cry for long times, not feeding you if you're having difficulty feeding, and sometimes being rough with you.

I struggle to find the words that explain how difficult for me it was to interview your mother.

Though it brought me agony, I gathered as much data as I could from your mother, from the nurses observing her, and from your medical records. I learned that your body had clear evidence of abuse, with bruises and broken bones. Not only were you neglected, you were also subjected to pain. I passed on the case to my supervisor respectfully.

May angels always protect you.

With gratitude,
Dr. Suhaila

Afterthoughts

Malak's mother's story filled me with frustration. On the one hand, I could imagine the hardships she went through. On the other hand, I found it difficult to speak to her when she showed no sadness or remorse towards Malak. I realized then that I was experiencing what doctors refer to as counter-transference. When negative emotional investment begins to seep into your mind towards a patient and it might consciously or subconsciously affect the way you see them. All physicians are taught to have a neutral mindset towards their patients; it's especially important for psychiatrists. Malak's story was a sad one, and it put me through an experience I always want to be aware of – that when countertransference happens and I started to have feelings of negativity towards her mother, admitting it and transferring care is the best for the patient, so that I wouldn't be biased when treating her. I now think of her mother in a neutral way, but I wonder about Malak frequently. I hope she knows that somebody out there feels for her struggle. Being a psychiatrist exposes me to plenty of cases that involve neglect and/or abuse. Throughout this career, I learned to hone my skills to be able to manage such cases, but it still breaks my heart every time.

WHAT IS NEGLECT, AND IS IT COMMON?

While violence or abuse is adding something, neglect is *withholding* something.

Though neglect in all age groups is a growing concern, the literature devoted to it is insufficient.[3] Since we discussed abuse in the adult population in the previous chapter, it's now worthwhile to turn our attention to child and elderly abuse.

Neglect is a form of maltreatment. Child maltreatment refers to "all types of physical and/or emotional ill-treatment, sexual abuse, neglect or negligent behavior, or commercial or other exploitation of children".[4] Elder abuse is defined as "a single, or repeated act, or lack of appropriate action, occurring within any relationship where there's an expectation of trust, which causes harm to the older person".[5]

A person might be subjected to neglect at any stage of their lives. A meta-analytic review showed that among children, 163 out of 1,000 suffer from physical neglect, and 184 out of 1,000 suffer from emotional neglect.[6] One study found that nearly one in 40 people over the age of 66 are subjected to abuse or neglect.[7] When it came to vulnerable adults (i.e. incapacitated in any way), a study found that one out of four vulnerable elderly are at risk of abuse.[8]

Here's a story highlighting how being elderly and having a mental disorder makes one susceptible to abuse.

Dear Fatima,

I hadn't even seen your face. It was through the COVID-19 pandemic, and we were recommending all the elderly patients to check in with us over the phone and send their children to pick up their medications. When I called you, you were reticent in your speech and disinterested in having a conversation. I asked what's the main thing that's bothering you, and you said that your son had taken away your parrot.

I then spoke to one of your sons; he informed me that one of your other sons had taken away your pet – the parrot. He told me that you fell back into a depression since. You developed a depressive disorder after losing your husband, and ever since, you've been in and out of depressive episodes. You found your comfort in a parrot, in a pet that you had taught to repeat back words to you. I wonder if you just wanted the company of a living thing that made you feel heard; maybe that's why you were so attached to the parrot.

Neglect

I tried to get more information out of you, but all you wanted to say was that "I know I'm old, I'm just waiting for the end...I lost my husband, I lost my pet companion and nobody in the world really understands me anymore". It broke my heart that it sounded like your children are attempting to minimize you and your needs, even when you particularly needed support. You were neglected, and so were your needs.

You made me think of my grandmother, and I could never imagine taking away anything that would make my grandmother feel less alone. I wished you were in front of me because I wanted to comfort you, and it's hard to do that over the phone. I wanted you to feel like as long as you were my patient, you were never alone.

Wherever you are now, I hope you have some sort of companionship.

With gratitude,
Dr. Suhaila

AFTERTHOUGHTS

Fatima loved her parrot. She loved how it repeated her husband's name, and it gave her somewhat of a connection to her life with her late husband. The elderly often complain of the pains of aging, but in my experience, they're more hesitant to describe mental ill-health. I kept wondering about age and how it affects us both physically and mentally. According to Erikson's stages of psychosocial development, Fatima was going through the conflict of integrity vs. despair,[9] and she had fallen deep into despair. This makes me reflect on the needs of the elderly, how they may be disadvantaged by ill physical health, but also how important it is not to neglect their mental wellbeing. I wondered what would have happened if this elderly lady was given a semblance of relief by having her parrot returned to her. Even if it didn't cure her depression, it would have given her the connection she craved. I could only hope that her sons would do right by her and bring back the one thing she had left connecting her to her late husband.

WHY ARE THE MENTALLY ILL MORE SUSCEPTIBLE TO NEGLECT?

People without mental illness might not have a hard time carrying out everyday tasks, whereas those with severe mental disorders may experience debilitating symptoms that lends them to being dependent. So those with a mental illness are likely to require assistance with daily activities and a reduced ability to tolerate stress or negative life experiences.[10] Their dependence could affect their caretaker and foster a sense of resentment, which could manifest as neglect.

It's sad to think about, but the perpetrators of abuse are often related to the survivor…as in "the people closest to you are most likely to hurt you". Studies proved that patients with a mental illness living with their families are likely to experience hostility from family members, which leads to relapses and hospitalization.[11]

Recall all the ways you interact with people to attain your daily needs. If you rely on your family members to fulfill them, what happens when they don't? And how does that situation affect someone with a pre-existing mental disorder? This is important to be aware of, because those with mental disorders and who are neglected aren't only denied their basic needs; they're also falling deeper into their disorder because neglect feeds into it.

Here's a story about a man with a mental disorder that shows how neglect leads to negative outcomes.

Dear Martin,

You're well into your thirties, but your father is still your primary caretaker because you suffer from a severe mental disorder. You're the patient who's notorious for having a problematic father. It's not only that your mental disorder is incapacitating, but also that your father neglects and abuses you. Your mother is out of the picture, so your father is all you have.

Every other month, your father finds himself incapable of taking care of you and he stops giving you your medications or checking on you. You're known to show up in the hospital when this happens. The challenge wasn't in dealing with you; it was in dealing with your father.

He supposedly pretends that he's keeping up with your mental disorder and medication regimen, but our tests show otherwise – that you're not taking your medications. To give your father the benefit of the doubt, this is either because you're refusing them, or he is neglecting to give them to you only so he would have a reason to bring you to the hospital to have you admitted...because he'd grown resentful of having to take care of you. The pattern of behavior supports the latter explanation.

Martin, you're the child of parents with a complicated relationship, you have a mental disorder, and you have scare resources to help you recover from that disorder. I once thought, "Where do we place the blame for Martin's deterioration?" – and I realized that the answer to this question is multi-faceted. You don't have a nuclear family for support, you have neglectful parents...but what I wish for you is that you'll always have physicians that recognize your misfortunes and hope that they do right by you.

With gratitude,
Dr. Suhaila

AFTERTHOUGHTS

It's difficult to think of Martin's situation and not feel upset. I think of a young man who could have had a life that was conducive in a way that managed his mental illness and added meaning to his life. This man, no longer a child, is still yearning for a regular family whereas he has a father that failed to provide him with a safe home and was constantly trying to pawn responsibility for him off to a psychiatric department in the hospital. And a psychiatric department in a hospital is unequal to a home. As a hospital, we treat those who are acutely ill…but a hospital is no place to live. To say that Martin should live in a psychiatric facility is reverting to the old ways of dealing with patients with a mental disorder – separate them from society and deny them any chance of a regular life, even if that life is not as normative as it is for those without a mental disorder.

I was not in a place to attempt to enforce mandates to keep him safe; all I could do is educate him, educate his father, and make sure that his environment is safe.

TAKEAWAYS

These stories show that no age or gender is immune to the effects of neglect.

Nobody deserves to be left alone or deprived of their basic needs, especially not those with a mental disorder. It can't be dismissed that anyone supporting someone with a mental illness has their own struggles; but that's no excuse to deprive them of support, love, and an open heart. Remember, people don't choose to have a mental disorder and it's hard enough to live with it; their mentality convinces them they are a burden…by neglecting them, it enforces the belief that they *are* a burden. Ultimately, you don't want your loved one to feel this way. Additionally, think of how differently you might act if somebody had a physical disability. If they had a broken leg, for example, you'd offer help with their daily needs – that's because it's a disorder that can be visualized with your own eyes. Don't forget about the disorders that aren't as visible, and that they're likely to need your support as well.

"Abuse and neglect negate love."

—BELL HOOKS

REFERENCES

1. Stoltenborgh, M., Bakermans-Kranenburg, M. J., & van IJzendoorn, M. H. (2012). The neglect of child neglect: a meta-analytic review of the prevalence of neglect. *Social Psychiatry and Psychiatric Epidemiology, 48*(3), 345–355. doi:10.1007/s00127-012-0549-y
2. Ibid.
3. Ibid.
4. Norman, R. E., Byambaa, M., De, R., Butchart, A., Scott, J., & Vos, T. (2012). The long-term health consequences of child physical abuse, emotional abuse, and neglect: a systematic review and meta-analysis. *PLoS Medicine, 9*(11), e1001349. doi:10.1371/journal.pmed.1001349
5. Simone, L., Wettstein, A., Senn, O., Rosemann, T., & Hasler, S. (2016). Types of abuse and risk factors associated with elder abuse. *Swiss Medical Weekly, 146*(0304), w14273. https://doi.org/10.4414/smw.2016.14273
6. Stoltenborgh, M., Bakermans-Kranenburg, M. J., & van IJzendoorn, M. H. (2012). The neglect of child neglect: a meta-analytic review of the prevalence of neglect. *Social Psychiatry and Psychiatric Epidemiology, 48*(3), 345–355. doi:10.1007/s00127-012-0549-y

7. Simone, L., Wettstein, A., Senn, O., Rosemann, T., & Hasler, S. (2016). Types of abuse and risk factors associated with elder abuse. *Swiss Medical Weekly, 146*(0304), w14273. https://doi.org/10.4414/smw.2016.14273
8. Cooper, C., Selwood, A., & Livingston, G. (2008). The prevalence of elder abuse and neglect: a systematic review. *Age and Ageing, 37*(2), 151–160. doi:10.1093/ageing/afm194
9. Simple Psychology. (2024, January 25). *Erik Erikson's Stages of Psychosocial Development.* Retrieved December 8, 2024, from https://www.simplypsychology.org/erik-erikson.html
10. Lamb, H. R. (1979). Roots of neglect of the long-term mentally ill. *Psychiatry, 42*(3), 201–207.
11. Ibid.

Chapter 7

MATERNAL MENTAL HEALTH

WHEN THERE ARE TWO PEOPLE TO WORRY ABOUT

Everyone says it takes a village to raise a child, but how often is it that anyone in that village is aware of the mental aspect of motherhood? You might have come across the term "baby blues" – this is when new mothers experience tearfulness and irritability, and it usually resolves within two weeks.[1]

However, mental disorders related to pregnancy and childbirth can be more serious.

Often, physical health is stressed during these times. Expecting mothers are reminded to take their prenatal vitamins, get regular check-ups, and pay additional attention to their overall wellbeing. While mental health might sometimes take a back seat, it should be stressed that it's part of overall wellbeing.

As a psychiatrist, I can attest to the statement above. During my rotation in the branch of psychiatry that liaises between psychiatry and other departments, I don't recall receiving a referral from obstetricians. The paucity of referrals is no measure for the prevalence of mental disorders in expecting or new mothers. In fact, a study in the United Arab Emirates found that 35% of women go through depressive symptoms six months postpartum.[2]

You always hear about a healthy pregnancy and delivery, but how often do we talk about when things go wrong for the child's mother?

To understand what I mean, here's a story illustrating those negative outcomes.

Dear Tamara,

I met you during my first week training in the obstetrics and gynecology department. I was assigned to the labor ward and I saw you walking back and forth in the hallway with your husband. You were sobbing, and I initially thought it was due to the pain. It was only later that my supervisor informed me that you had carried this baby to full term but the baby was deceased. You refused surgery, and you decided to give birth naturally to a baby that you weren't even going to get to keep.

As you went back and forth, I asked to be assigned to your treating team. My supervisor looked at me stunned and said, "Why would you want to work on a team that has a patient who is bound to deteriorate?". She sneered at me and accused me of not choosing to be on the team that had ample opportunities to learn. I explained how it wouldn't be beneficial for me to only go about seeing healthy pregnancies and deliveries, but that I could gain even more experience if I also dealt with the failures.

To my surprise, I was assigned to a different team and it happened to be your treating team the next day. I asked the team if they considered referring you to a mental health team; they responded, "Why? Do you think she's showing signs of mental illness?". So, I replied, "No, but she just went through an experience that exhausted her body, not to mention the impact on her mental wellbeing – she needs support". My supervisor was unhappy, because having to call for a referral would be adding to her workload. And she said to me, "You go and talk to her after we finish our rounds, get all the information we need to refer her to a mental health professional, write it up, send it to me and I'll relay it to the mental health team".

I was nervous to talk to you; what words can encompass the sorrow with having a still childbirth? I spoke to you about your job, your husband, and your family. At that moment, I wasn't your doctor, I wasn't even your psychiatrist...I was just a woman having a conversation with another woman. When it came to the hard part, asking you about how your mental status was, you kept quiet. Though I could see you were about to cry, I didn't want to push you to a point where I couldn't help you. After all, I wasn't a psychiatrist yet...I was only an intern. You might've not shared with me your recent struggle, but I'd like to think of our conversation as a relief from having to talk about the traumatic event you had just gone through.

I wasn't assigned to the department long enough to know how things turned out for you, but I say a prayer every time I remember you – that you're living a happy life with a healthy family, your husband, and the three children you always wanted.

With gratitude,
Dr. Suhaila

Afterthoughts

Every time I think of Tamara, I think about how healthcare systems often fail to communicate the need to provide all aspects of care to the people who trust us with their health. It shocked me that I was asked why this patient would need to be referred to a mental health professional. My supervisors informed me that they only refer patients who go through severe mental disorders that pose a safety risk to them and their children. But what about the people like Tamara?

What about those who don't show obvious signs of a mental disorder, but go through something so traumatic? I felt disappointed that the doctors only attended to her physical issues, but nobody other than me was talking about the mental torment. How can a woman go through a full pregnancy, the pain of labor, to have it end in the tragedy of a deceased child? That in itself is a cause for grief. This experience taught me that we need to commiserate with our patients, even if their struggles are foreign to us.

WHAT IS MATERNAL MENTAL HEALTH?

Everyone stands to benefit from knowledge about maternal mental health, whether you're a healthcare professional or a layperson. This is because the nature of these disorders might cause harm to a pregnant lady or to a new mother and her newborn child.

The word "peripartum" refers to the time before, during and after birth. As mentioned above, postpartum blues differs from disorders like postpartum depression. Some of the severe peripartum mental disorders include depressive disorder, bipolar disorder, and psychotic disorders.[3]

Some women might have pre-existing mental disorders that may flare up when they're pregnant, while others might experience these disorders in the peripartum period. Both scenarios are important to recognize, as there are consequences if they're not treated. For example, a study showed that women with untreated depressive symptoms during pregnancy are likely to poorly utilize prenatal clinics, misuse substances, and have preterm delivery with low birth weight.[4] So for women with depressive disorder, the risk of discontinuing medications during pregnancy has negative outcomes for both the mother and her baby.

The upcoming story touches on these issues.

Dear Shamsa,

Six weeks after you gave birth, your husband brought you to the emergency department stating that you're unwell. You didn't know your husband brought you for a psychiatric assessment; you thought he was taking you to one of your postnatal check-ups. When I spoke to you, you were irritable, restless and unhappy to be in the hospital. I asked if you had ever been diagnosed with a mental disorder, and you responded: "I used to have some issues but I'm alright now, I don't even need my medications anymore".

I inquired about your symptoms; you mentioned sleeplessness as well as changes in your mood but you kept attributing it to being in the postpartum stage. You spoke about your newborn, who was born prematurely after a complicated labor. Your main concern was getting back to your baby girl; you stated that you felt intensely guilty because you haven't been able to bond with her. You placed the blame on yourself for being overwhelmed, you started to cry and asked, "Why can't I be a good mother?".

Your husband told us that your mood has been fluctuating between sadness and anxiety and that you hadn't been eating or sleeping well. He understood that you were going through depression. He mentioned that you were diagnosed years ago, that you'd been stable with medications but you stopped taking them when you got pregnant without consulting your treating psychiatrist.

For your own and your baby's safety, my supervisor and I decided that you should stay in the hospital. You cried all the time, lamenting over being separated from your baby...it was agonizing to witness. We couldn't force you to take medications, but we negotiated with you that if you wanted to leave the hospital, you had to let us find a way to help you. For days, you refused medications until one day when you asked, "Will I be a good mother if I take the medications?". So we had a long discussion about postpartum depression, and we explained to you that the feelings of guilt and inadequacy, combined with your mood, appetite, and sleep issues were all symptoms of a disorder. You then admitted that you went through depressive episodes before, but not like this. Since this was your first baby, you weren't aware that stopping your medications could bring about a relapse or the complications that could arise as a result.

Ten days passed; you were sleeping and eating better. You were engaging more with improved concentration. Most importantly, you were amenable to taking medications and you understood their importance. You were finally stable enough to leave the hospital.

As you were about to leave you said, "I used to be anxious about my baby, but now I'm excited to be a mother".

With gratitude,
Dr. Suhaila

AFTERTHOUGHTS

Sometimes it's hard for those with depressive disorder to accept that their symptoms aren't their own fault. With depressive mothers, there's the added guilt of inadequacy. Shamsa's story is a typical example of this, embodying the consequences of discontinuing medications. However, it's also a story of hope, recovery, and the importance of having social support. Shamsa went back to her baby girl with a newfound excitement when her depression was managed and continued to follow up with mental health services. It was a pleasure to be part of her story.

***

Pregnancy is considered a blessing, but what happens when it's unintended?

Different countries vary when it comes to unintended pregnancy, but it's estimated that 80 million unplanned pregnancies happen annually worldwide.[5] It's important to note that unintended pregnancies can be wanted or unwanted, either due to being mistimed or due to the lack of desire to have children in the first place.

Studies show that women with unwanted pregnancies have higher levels of depressive symptoms. Women who become pregnant after they think they're done with childbearing are likely to suffer health issues, because raising children poses social and economic burdens[6] as you'll read in the story below.

Dear Ameera,

Your husband brought you to the emergency department; you were pale, vomiting, anxious and in pain. My first guess is that you might have a stomach bug. You were also concerned that you had appendicitis because some of your siblings had it. We sent out your investigations and I remembered to add in a pregnancy test as we do for all women of childbearing age. While waiting for the results, we gave you fluids and painkillers. Your results showed a hormone level correlating to pregnancy. I went to my supervisor and asked, "Can I be the one to tell her? I've never told a patient she was pregnant before," and she agreed.

I came back to see how you were feeling after the treatment was administered, and I told you that you're pregnant. To my surprise, you were displeased. You said that you already have three children and you're not ready for another pregnancy, then you cried. You still seemed ill and pale, so I examined you again and you still winced from pain at the slightest touch. Something seemed off to me. I called my supervising consultant to see you and she agreed to let me do an abdominal ultrasound which should show a pregnant uterus but no sac (no signs of a baby). According to her hormone level, this should be visible in the sixth week of pregnancy.

At this point, both my consultant and I left to try to find a physician with some experience in obstetrics in the emergency department while wondering if we should shift you to a specialized hospital for obstetrics and gynecology. Another colleague joined us. We came back to your room to find that your blood pressure was dropping and a more thorough ultrasound shows that there are collections of fluid in your abdomen – this indicated that you were experiencing an ectopic pregnancy. Your diagnosis quickly shifted from a stomach bug to ectopic pregnancy and internal bleeding. I believe the term "OR STAT" was said while I was standing there stunned.

You were worried about an unwanted pregnancy and I wondered how you felt that within minutes of finding out, you were being wheeled into the operating room to terminate it. Was there some temporary relief that you didn't have to go through with the pregnancy? And how did that mix into the anxiety of suddenly being told that you had to undergo major surgery? Your room in the emergency department had already been emptied and replaced with a clean bed before I could find out.

I remember your husband's initial reaction about the pregnancy before we did the ultrasound – he smiled. And when you said you weren't ready for it, he said: "I'm the positive one, she's negative but opposites attract".

Ameera, I will not forget you, your husband, and the spirit lost that you may or may not mourn; I know I will.

With gratitude,
Dr. Suhaila

AFTERTHOUGHTS

Even though I'm a psychiatrist, part of my training was to spend some time in the emergency department. Due to some complications that happened during the COVID-19 pandemic, I ended up training in emergency later than I expected. If that hadn't happened, I wouldn't have encountered Ameera. For that, I'm humbled as a physician. I kept thinking what I could have done differently, Could I have done a more thorough abdominal examination and detected the internal bleeding earlier? I was hesitant because Ameera was in pain whenever she was examined. Retrospectively, I know that this woman was in more pain than she was showing. And this is what happens when a psychiatrist works in the emergency department – even when treating physical illnesses, a patient's mental distress is always on our minds. I keep thinking, should her pallor have alerted me earlier, should I have started to worry when her pain didn't subside after receiving painkillers? I realize now that what should've alerted me was my gut feeling that I couldn't examine her abdomen without her retracting with pain, the second I knew something was off but couldn't quite put my finger on it (pun intended). It reminded me to trust my instinct earlier. I don't want to forget the version of me who came to that conclusion.

Takeaways

Childbearing and childbirth are wonderful things, but we need to pay more attention to how that affects mothers. Because while there are two people to worry about, mental health needs to be considered. Women often don't talk about pregnancy complications, miscarriages or a stillbirth. But why is that? Why do we shame women for negative outcomes of pregnancy when most of the time, it's no way their fault? Women find it difficult to disclose such information as they risk negative judgements, insensitive comments or others trivializing their experience.[7] Now obviously, there are cultural considerations when it comes to talking about pregnancy and everything that relates to it. But does that mean that we shouldn't talk about when things go wrong?

It's heart-wrenching to me to think of all the women out there who've suffered like Tamara and Ameera, and my hope is that reading these stories will encourage anyone who has been through similar experiences to seek help. It doesn't have to be in the form of announcing your struggle; it can be as simple as taking one day a week to speak to a therapist or calling someone you confide in and saying, "Hey, I've gone through something that traumatized me, and I need help". Studies show that disclosing traumatizing events improves mental health.[8]

Trust me, help is available, and I know it for sure because I constantly try to put myself in situations where I can be helpful, just like with Tamara, Shamsa and Ameera. Child-bearing and motherhood can be mentally stressful. I can only wish that I've relayed that to you through these women's stories. On the other hand, a mother's love for her child can at any point become a protective factor and an enormous source of strength – that's why we keep hoping.

> *"Those we have held in our arms for a little while, we hold in our hearts forever."*
>
> —Khalil Gibran

References

1. Woody, C. A., Ferrari, A. J., Siskind, D. J., Whiteford, H. A., & Harris, M. G. (2017). A systematic review and meta-regression of the prevalence and incidence of perinatal depression. *Journal of Affective Disorders,* 219, 86–92. doi:10.1016/j.jad.2017.05.003
2. Hanach, N., Radwan, H., Fakhry, R., Dennis, C. L., Issa, W. B., Faris, M. E., ... & De Vries, N. (2023). Prevalence and risk factors of postpartum depression among women living in the United Arab Emirates. *Social Psychiatry and Psychiatric Epidemiology, 58*(3), 395–407.
3. Kalra, H., Tran, T., Romero, L., Chandra, P., & Fisher, J. (2022). Burden of severe maternal peripartum mental disorders in low- and middle-income countries: a systematic

review. *Archives of Women's Mental Health, 25*(2), 267–275.

4. Evans, J., Heron, J., Francomb, H., Oke, S., & Golding, J. (2001). Cohort study of depressed mood during pregnancy and after childbirth. *BMJ (Clinical research ed.), 323*(7307), 257–260. https://doi.org/10.1136/bmj.323.7307.257

5. Ali A. (2016). Relationship between unwanted pregnancy and health-related quality of life in pregnant women. *Journal of the College of Physicians and Surgeons – Pakistan, 26*(6), 507–512.

6. Herd, P., Higgins, J., Sicinski, K., & Merkurieva, I. (2016). The implications of unintended pregnancies for mental health in later life. *American Journal of Public Health, 106*(3), 421–429. https://doi.org/10.2105/AJPH.2015.302973

7. Bute, J., Brann, M. & Hernandez, R. (2019). Exploring societal-level privacy rules for talking about miscarriage. *Journal of Social and Personal Relationships,* 36, 379–399. 10.1177/0265407517731828.

8. Petronio, S. (2002). *Boundaries of privacy: Dialectics of disclosure.* Albany, NY: State University of New York Press.

Chapter 8

MEN'S MENTAL HEALTH

WHAT HAPPENS WHEN BOYS DON'T CRY

Men are brought up in a way that makes them believe they need to be superhuman and show no weakness, thereby they may view emotional display as a sign of weakness. Studies support this as men who self-identify as being strongly self-reliant had 34% greater odds of reporting suicidal thoughts.[1] Additionally, men have a belief that disorders like depression should be managed alone.[2]

WHAT MAKES MEN VULNERABLE?

Men's mental issues stem from the way they cope with psychological distress. Depression, substance abuse, and suicide in men are the result of maladaptive coping.[3] Additionally, it has been posed that symptoms of depression in men differ from the standard criteria. Though not yet diagnostically considered, there are externalizing behaviors such as anger, alcohol abuse and risk-taking that point to depression.[4]

You are about to read a story that highlights this statement.

Dear Mark,

You attended the emergency department for chest pain, and after the emergency doctors worked you up, they found no evidence of a serious physical illness and it turned out you were having a panic attack. I happened to be in the department consulting on another case when one of my colleagues came up to me and said, "I won't make this an official consultation since the patient is refusing to follow up with psychiatry, but could you do me a favor and counsel him? He seems really distressed, he mentioned alcohol use and you will probably be able to get more out of him than I did". I agreed to see you.

I walked in to find a well-dressed gentleman sitting up in a chair. "Are you Mr. Mark?" I asked. You responded, "Yes that's me". I asked why you weren't lying on the hospital bed; you said that there was no reason to since you are well. I explained to you that I'm from the mental health team and I'm here for a little chat if it's okay with you. Suddenly, your hands started to shake, and you were fiddling in your chair as though distressed by my presence or request to discuss your mental wellbeing. From the looks of it, you were having another panic attack but refused to admit it. So instead of trying to convince you of it, I started to do breathing exercises with you.

Once you calmed down, you started telling me about the difficult circumstances you were in. Your wife had left you, sued you for custody of your children, and travelled back to your home country.

You had to stay here because of your job contract, and work wasn't going so well because you had a hard time concentrating when it felt like your life was falling apart. You were barely making ends meet, what with the expenses of living and having to pay alimony. I asked how you've been coping, and you said, "I have a glass of wine to calm my nerves almost every night or whenever I get these episodes". You were reluctant to call your episodes panic attacks – that would've been admitting that you had a mental health issue. I must've spent 45 minutes listening to you talk about your symptoms but attributing them to a physical issue. I explained to you the nature of panic attacks, taught you breathing exercises, and offered you appointments with mental health services. You adamantly refused. All I could do was reassure you and offer help. I wrote down a list of places to seek help for mental health issues including alcohol use and gave it to you. I couldn't predict what was going to happen or what you'd do after I left, but I kept hoping that maybe something I said would resonate with you and you'd reach out.

Wherever you are now Mark, I hope you're happily remarried, I hope you're doing well at your job,

I hope you get to see your children often...I really hope you're well.

With gratitude,
Dr. Suhaila

AFTERTHOUGHTS

The day I met Mark, I was accompanied by an intern whom it was my job to teach. After we left the room, she asked, "Aren't you going to make sure he follows up?". I could sense that she had that lingering feeling of helplessness – which is an experience I know all too well. I asked her what she would do if the decision was hers to make, and she had no response. I explained to her what my supervisors had said to me before: "Sometimes, helping is just by listening". "But he has panic attacks, and he consumes alcohol; shouldn't we admit him to the hospital?" my intern asked. I told her that our job is to ensure the patient's safety, educate, counsel, and reiterate that we're always here to provide help. I explained to her that as long as he's of sound mind with the capacity to understand the consequences of his actions, the options available, and the benefits and risks of his condition, it's not up to us to force help on him. Whether or not patients choose to accept it is their decision. That was the principle of autonomy – and we had no right or legitimate reason to take away Mark's choice, even if it broke our hearts.

BARRIERS TO SEEKING HELP

The unrealistic expectations that are placed on men make them vulnerable to mental disorders; those are the same expectations that pose limitations to seeking help. To understand this, think of the meaning of masculinity. Traditional masculinity includes a set of norms that highlight certain expressions.[5] These may include self-control, stoicism, and invulnerability.[6] Young males often show aggression or violence – we see it in how they "play rough" – and this is deemed acceptable.[7] However, that plays into how these young males grow to think of emotional expression.

Stigma also has a role when it comes to expressing emotion or seeking help. Stigma could be social, perceived, professional, or cultural. And those with mental health issues are seen as "weak, broken, not strong enough".[8] The accumulation of stigma from various sources is considered a barrier. No man wants to perceive himself as weak or broken, let alone have the people around him see him that way. It's almost verboten for a man to declare that he requires professional help in dealing with emotions.

Men who aren't taught or allowed to express and manage their emotions can't be entirely healthy. Masculinity values logic more than emotion, but that doesn't negate the presence of emotion. Dismissing emotion is like throwing away a piece of a puzzle, which wouldn't be complete that way. When it comes to making fully rounded decisions, whether at home or in the workplace, emotion should be factored in to an extent.

Problems arise when toxic ideals of masculinity are held strongly. As such ideals enforce certain behaviors – like crying or being afraid – are viewed as unacceptable.[9] There are risks to holding that belief, especially for men who live with a mental disorder. Below is a story of a man who deteriorated due to masculine norms.

Dear Rashid,

I met you when you were hospitalized; you already had a diagnosis of bipolar disorder. You lived with your mother, and you were compliant with your management plan. But recently you were visited by your father, who lives with his second family. Your father convinced you that you don't have a mental disorder and shouldn't be taking medications, so you stopped taking them.

When we attempted to interview you, you wouldn't stop talking about how you quit your job because of your plans to start your own company, how you were going to invest all your savings, and that you were sure you were going to be a billionaire. It was clear you were in a manic episode.

Your father arrived later that day, a stern man who insisted for you to be discharged from the hospital. Your father said, "We don't have any crazy people in the family". When we asked him how he would explain what you're going through, he replied, "Whenever Rashid acts in this manner, we know his possession returned, he's not in touch with his faith, and he has a weak personality". While it was not our place to argue about your father's personal faith and beliefs regarding possession, we tried to educate him about bipolar disorder, but he wasn't convinced.

The next day, we met your mother. She told us about your diagnosis, and that she understands it's a mental disorder because your uncle has the same condition. Even though she didn't like the idea of you being hospitalized, she agreed that your condition needed to be stabilized with medications. "Rashid was always intelligent and creative, but when he gets these episodes, he acts irrationally and impulsively," your mother told us. "It doesn't help that his father is always so stern with him". She explained how you've quit jobs three times, and she was worried you'd be financially unstable one day due to your impulsivity.

We spoke to her about what your father said, and how his opinions might get in the way of you getting better because he wants you out of the hospital. She informed us that she would discuss this with your father – who arrived shortly. We interviewed you with your parents to discuss how to proceed with your management. Your mother managed to convince your father to let us keep you in the hospital, but your father said, "We're not telling anyone he's in a mental hospital, what would people think of us?" and your mother responded, "We won't, but we'll keep him here until he's stable". Your father looked at you and said, "Toughen up and be a man so you can get out of here".

As your mother was leaving, she looked back at us and said, "This is my firstborn, he's my pride, keep him safe".

*With gratitude,
Dr. Suhaila*

AFTERTHOUGHTS

Rashid's story is a very common occurrence. Sometimes a family's attitudes towards mental disorder hinder a patient's recovery; in this case, it was compounded by Rashid's father's attitude about masculinity. What his father said implied that being a man means having a strong personality and not being afflicted by mental turmoil. Both his parents were educated people, but it was only his mother who had more awareness of his disorder. I felt extremely glad that someone in his family supports his treatment. Otherwise, what would have happened to Rashid?

※

What happens to men who are always told to 'man up'?

Emotions exist, and there are consequences of not adequately addressing them. Studies show that men who fixate on masculinity have negative outcomes including worsening of psychological distress or mental disorders, substance abuse, and interpersonal and relationship issues.[10] Men might minimize their emotions, but that doesn't mean that they don't display them in other ways, like using defense mechanisms. These mechanisms are often unconscious, and we utilize them to protect ourselves from discomfort. Some of these mechanisms are considered mature, but most are classified as immature. It is worthwhile to note that these mechanisms are used both by men and women, however they are highlighted here for their relevance to stories in this chapter. Below is a table explaining these mechanisms (adapted from Ganti et al., 2016, pp. 180–182).[11]

Defense mechanism		Explanation
Immature	Acting out	Giving in to an inappropriate impulse to avoid the stress of suppressing that impulse
	Denial	Refusing to accept a reality that's too painful
	Regression	Returning to an earlier stage of development to avoid the stress associated with the current developmental stage
	Projection	Attributing personal thoughts or emotions to others
	Splitting	Believing things are all good or all bad (no in-between)
	Undoing	Performing a behavior to attempt to reverse a situation
	Displacement	Behavior or emotion redirected to another person
	Controlling	Attempting to regulate external environment to relieve stress
	Intellectualization	Avoiding negative feelings by focusing on intellectual functions
	Isolation of affect	Absence of an emotional response towards an uncomfortable reality
	Rationalization	Using justifications or excuses for an event or behavior to make it more acceptable
	Reaction formation	Doing the opposite of an unacceptable behavior

Defense mechanism		Explanation
Mature	Repression	Preventing thoughts or feelings from entering consciousness (unlike suppression, repression is unconscious)
	Altruism	Engaging in acts that help others to vicariously relieve stress
	Humor	Dealing with stress by seeing irony in a situation
	Sublimation	Turning maladaptive impulses to unacceptable behavior
	Suppression	Avoid thinking about stressors until they can be dealt with
	Affiliation	Turning to others for support

There are more tragic outcomes than the ones described above. In the face of unsolvable issues, men might feel helpless and that puts them at risk for suicide.[12] Suicide in men has been described as a 'silent epidemic'.[13] One study found that suicide is among the top three causes of death in males between the ages of 15 and 44, and men are 3 to 7.5 times more likely to die by suicide than woman.[14] These numbers should be alarming enough to warrant interventions to ensure men's mental wellbeing and prevent them losing their lives.

Takeaways

There's a growing body of literature regarding men's mental health, yet there's still a lack of awareness when it comes to what should be done. What I hope you take away from this chapter is that we need to replace the notion of toxic masculinity with *positive* masculinity. When a man seeks professional help, he becomes a role model for his entire gender. Change needs to happen at every level: parents should tell boys that they are allowed to cry, and alert them as to how that helps them process emotions. Men should have a safe space to properly communicate their feelings, without judgement from their family or friends. And healthcare professionals also play a role in this by exploring the complexity of treating male patients.

If we consider men to be the pillars of society, imagine the profound impact it would have if they were allowed to express basic human emotions, and be mentally well.

"Manhood needs to be redefined."

—Benita N. Chatmon

REFERENCES

1. Pirkis, J., Spittal, M. J., Keogh, L., Mousaferiadis, T., & Currier, D. (2017). Masculinity and suicidal thinking. *Social Psychiatry and Psychiatric Epidemiology, 52*, 319–327.
2. Rice, S. M., Aucote, H. M., Parker, A. G., Alvarez-Jimenez, M., Filia, K. M., & Amminger, G. P. (2017). Men's perceived barriers to help seeking for depression: Longitudinal findings relative to symptom onset and duration. *Journal of Health Psychology, 22*(5), 529–536.
3. Bilsker, D., Fogarty, A. S., & Wakefield, M. A. (2018). Critical issues in men's mental health. *The Canadian Journal of Psychiatry, 63*(9), 590–596.
4. Addis, M. E. (2008). Gender and depression in men. *Clinical Psychology: Science and Practice, 15*(3), 153.
5. Chatmon, B. N. (2020). Males and mental health stigma. *American Journal of Men's Health, 14*(4), 1557988320949322.
6. Rice, S. M., Aucote, H. M., Parker, A. G., Alvarez-Jimenez, M., Filia, K. M., & Amminger, G. P. (2017). Men's perceived barriers to help seeking for depression:

Longitudinal findings relative to symptom onset and duration. *Journal of Health Psychology, 22*(5), 529–536.

7. Chatmon, B. N. (2020). Males and mental health stigma. *American Journal of Men's Health, 14*(4), 1557988320949322.
8. Ibid.
9. Ibid.
10. Ibid.
11. Ganti, L., Kaufman, M. S., & Blitzstein, S. (2016). *First aid for the psychiatry clerkship* (4th ed., pp. 180–182). McGraw-Hill Education/Medical.
12. Bilsker, D., Fogarty, A. S., & Wakefield, M. A. (2018). Critical issues in men's mental health. *The Canadian Journal of Psychiatry, 63*(9), 590–596.
13. Bell, D. (2010). *The silent epidemic of male suicide.* Bbc.co.uk; BBC. http://news.bbc.co.uk/2/hi/uk_news/7219232.stm
14. Rice, S. M., Aucote, H. M., Parker, A. G., Alvarez-Jimenez, M., Filia, K. M., & Amminger, G. P. (2017). Men's perceived barriers to help seeking for depression: Longitudinal findings relative to symptom onset and duration. *Journal of Health Psychology, 22*(5), 529–536.

Chapter 9

ANXIETY DISORDERS

FEAR: FRIEND OR FOE?

Try to bring to your mind a memory of a situation when you felt afraid, then try to remember how your body reacted. Was it merely mental? Or did your heart start to race? Did you feel like the stress chemical epinephrine was flooding your circulation? Did you start to feel short of breath and almost paralyzed? That's anxiety.

Anxiety could be experienced by any one of us. While the symptom of anxiety is found in many disorders,[1] anxiety disorder is considered by the World Health Organization to be the most common mental disorder. An estimated 300 million people globally are living with it, yet only one in four people are treated for it.[2]

THE ORIGINS OF FEAR AND ANXIETY

The words 'fear' and 'anxiety' are sometimes used interchangeably. While they may overlap, the distinction is that fear is usually an emotional response to an imminent threat. Both fear and anxiety could be thought of as having an evolutionary basis and manifesting physically. Specific fears are typical at certain ages, and they often wane with time, as the table below shows (adapted from Muris & Field, 2011).[3]

Age	Normal expected fear
0–6 months	Falls, loud noise
6–12 months	Strangers, sudden unexpected objects

Age	Normal expected fear
1 year	Strangers, parental separation
2–3 years	Dark, animals, thunder
5–8 years	Supernatural creatures
9–12 years	Physical injuries, natural disasters
Adolescence	Social evaluation

The fight or flight response to fear is a well-known phenomenon that occurs in the face of a threatening stimulus. What happens when it seems to occur out of nowhere? The reality is that it has to do with anticipating a future threat. What defines anxiety as a disorder is when it becomes excessive and inconsistent with developmentally normative reactions – as you'll find out in the story below.

Dear Khalid,

You attended the clinic complaining that your entire life has been affected by your fear of driving over bridges. You expressed your frustration at feeling like you are "unable to do something so basic". We spoke for quite some time, and I had come to find out that your anxiety was regarding one specific thing – otherwise known as a specific phobia. I asked you what it is exactly that brought on your anxiety; you responded that you were worried the bridge would collapse or that you would accidentally drive off it (even though you'd never experienced such a thing). I wanted to know how you cope with it; you stated that you have to take frequent detours on your way to work to avoid bridges, which prolongs your journey, and that you avoid social situations in locations that require you to drive over a bridge.

"What happens if you have no option but to drive over a bridge?" I asked. You told me about how your heart races, you feel like you can't see straight, your extremities begin to feel numb, and you keep thinking you might die. You mentioned that any time you must, you end up parking your car on the side of the road until your anxiety subsides.

Most men wait until their mental health issues become debilitating to seek help, and so did you. Despite that, I was glad you finally decided that your condition requires professional help. We agreed that your condition requires treatment with medications, therapy and social support.

The next time you attended the clinic, you spoke about how you'd become more hopeful regarding overcoming your phobia. You had to make adjustments to your life, but we still had to identify which adjustments were feeding into your phobia and which were helping you overcome it. You decided to stop driving and hired a driver, but you also started going to therapy to overcome your phobia.

Even though the last time I saw you, you hadn't achieved remission...you were on your way by making minor changes in different aspects. I will always be glad that you were taking those small steps to recovery.

*With gratitude,
Dr. Suhaila*

Afterthoughts

There was an element of positivity when it came to Khalid's story. It's often difficult for men to seek professional help. It was too bad that Khalid waited until his condition got this bad to attend a clinic, but he eventually did and found a path to getting better. His situation was one of the most severe forms of phobia I've encountered, and it taught me never to dismiss the large impact specific phobias and panic disorder can have on a patient's life.

Classifying anxiety disorders

There are various types of anxiety disorders as classified by the DSM-5, which include generalized anxiety disorder, separation anxiety disorder, selective mutism, social phobia, panic disorder, agoraphobia, specific phobia, and others.[4]

The upcoming story is one that first made me aware of selective mutism.

Dear Sharifa,

One day, we were visiting a health and educational center for the differently abled. It was during my days in medical college. I had not yet rotated in the psychiatry department, but part of my college's curriculum is to visit centers in underserved communities.

Other children and adolescents had obvious disorders that explained their enrollment in such a center, but you were an anomaly amongst them. At the age of 10, you stopped speaking in school. There seemed to be no physical reason for this; you didn't have any visual or hearing impairments. This happened after you had already achieved your language milestones, so it was not a developmental disorder. It didn't seem warranted for you to be attending this center, yet due to the scarcity of resources in your community, that's where you ended up.

We learned of your story through your mother. She told us that at the start of the new academic year, you attended a regular school, but you weren't engaging or speaking to your teachers or classmates. Your mother had to withdraw you from that school as you were deemed by the administration as unfit to attend. Your mother appeared overprotective, and she informed us that you prefer to speak to your father through voice recordings and that you clung to him when he was around. She couldn't understand why you refused to speak in certain situations; she had no idea that your condition is a mental disorder.

You sat quietly as your mother spoke and had a downward gaze, only looking up from time to time but specifically when your father was mentioned. The entire time we spent with you, we never heard your voice.

As a student, I was in these situations for learning purposes. I had no certification yet that enabled me to be part of your care. I pray that you were eventually given the proper care and that you found your voice again.

With gratitude,
Dr. Suhaila

Afterthoughts

Sharifa's story alerted me to a relatively rare anxiety disorder and truly made me aware of the complexities of managing it. I kept thinking, how do you get information from a patient who wouldn't speak to you? What could have possibly happened to her that she reached this stage? Also, how do you help someone who's misplaced in a community where there's inadequate mental healthcare awareness and care? The interaction with her reminded me of the importance of observing behavior when it comes to mental health issues. Throughout my career, I didn't encounter another patient with selective mutism. However, while training to become a psychiatrist, I drew on Sharifa's story so that if I ever do meet someone like her, I'll be better equipped to help them.

Physical disorder or anxiety disorder?

Many people attend the emergency department complaining of physical symptoms like headaches, back or shoulder aches, dizziness, shortness of breath, and heart palpitations, believing those symptoms are due to a physical illness. When questioned further, they might disclose symptoms that allude to an anxiety disorder. These usually include persistent and generalized worries, irritability, difficulty concentrating, and sleep disturbances,[5] as was the case with the next story.

Dear Fatima,

As an elderly patient, when you attend the emergency department, the doctors usually investigate you for physical causes of your concerns. At some point, you started attending the emergency department so often that the emergency doctors were convinced that your ailments are psychological.

When I was called to see you, I reviewed your file and found out that you were diagnosed with generalized anxiety disorder, and you developed a dependence on anti-anxiety medications. Normally, these medications are used short-term until psychotherapeutic interventions help alleviate the symptoms of anxiety.

Despite counselling, you didn't attend therapy. Your children were growing weary of attempting to quell your anxiety and having to take care of you. It turned out that you had been taking more of your medications than prescribed, so when you couldn't find a pill to help with your anxiety, you asked your children to bring you to the hospital.

When it comes to ways of coping, yours was maladaptive. You were convinced that there's nothing that can help except anti-anxiety medications. Your presence in the hospital became too frequent, and you always demanded the same medications.

It must've been horrendous to continuously experience anxiety and feel like there's no sort of antidote that helps. I hope you find a good coping mechanism and I hope you find safety.

With gratitude,
Dr. Suhaila

Afterthoughts

This is a patient I've encountered multiple times during my training. Every time, it was a bigger challenge as it felt like repeating the same advice that the patient would say she understood but did not go by. I only wished that there was a way to get through to her. When the people around her started to feel fed up, she would find solace in being at the hospital and she was convinced there was only one way for her to feel better – medications. While others might have judged her, I couldn't help but think of her helplessness. It reminded me of my helplessness towards her. Eventually, I had to accept that I had exhausted my options of helping this patient the way I assumed I needed to. It was difficult to make peace with it, but the fact of the matter is, there's only so much we can do.

Takeaways

I hope the stories in this chapter alerted you to the different kinds of anxiety disorders that people go through and how they can manifest. The next time you have a physical ailment with no explanation, maybe you'll wonder if the origin is psychological. This isn't to say that physical symptoms should be ignored, but there are classifications of anxiety disorders that should be considered if all physical investigations are normal. The anguish that comes with anxiety results from feelings of losing control of your thoughts and causes great suffering.[6] It's greatly distressful for those who experience it for a short period of time, so it's understandable that those who have it as a disorder find it debilitating to their lives.

> *"Perhaps all anxiety might derive from a fixation on moments – an inability to accept life as ongoing."*
>
> —Sarah Manguso

References

1. Harrison, P., Cowen, P., Burns, T., & Fazel, M. (2017). Anxiety and obsessive-compulsive disorders. In *Shorter Oxford Textbook of Psychiatry* (7th ed., pp. 161–170). https://doi.org/10.1093/med/9780198747437.001.0001
2. World Health Organization: WHO. (2023, September 27). *Anxiety disorders.* https://www.who.int/news-room/fact-sheets/detail/anxiety-disorders
3. Muris, P., & P. Field, A. (2011). The "normal" development of fear. In W. K. Silverman & A. P. Field (Eds.), *Anxiety Disorders in Children and Adolescents* (pp. 76–89). Cambridge: Cambridge University Press.
4. American Psychiatric Association. (2022). Anxiety disorders. In *Diagnostic and Statistical Manual of Mental Disorders* (5th ed., text rev.).

5. Harrison, P., Cowen, P., Burns, T., & Fazel, M. (2017). Anxiety and obsessive-compulsive disorders. In *Shorter Oxford Textbook of Psychiatry* (7th ed., pp. 161–170). https://doi.org/10.1093/med/9780198747437.001.0001
6. Wittchen, H.-U. (2002). Generalized anxiety disorder: prevalence, burden, and cost to society. *Depression and Anxiety, 16*(4), 162–171. doi:10.1002/da.10065

Chapter 10

SUBSTANCE USE DISORDERS

HABIT OR DISORDER?

Most of us have something that we can't go about our day without – like a cup of coffee, or maybe a certain food – which is to say that we're all addicted to something.

At some point, what people become dependent on could harm them and put their health at risk. Some types of risky addictions have become socially acceptable as they're legal, like smoking cigarettes. Other types of risky addictions are less accepted as the substances are illegal.

WHAT YOU THINK YOU CAN CONTROL CAN EVENTUALLY CONTROL YOU

I've had a university professor refer to addiction as a sort of psychological slavery. This is how he explained it: The concept of slavery captures the essence of the modern-day understanding of addiction, because it shows that pursuit has moved beyond voluntary control.

To refer to the subtitle of this book, is addiction a habit or a disorder? When a harmful substance takes hold of your life, to the point of not being able to function a day without it…it's a disorder.

For the sake of removing bias, I'll be referring to addiction as substance use disorder (SUD) moving forward in this chapter. Here's a story about a young man whose dependence ultimately cost him deeply.

Dear Hamad,

You started using substances to improve your performance; you were talking about how stressed you felt regarding your parents' expectations of you. You had a hard time concentrating on your studies, and a friend suggested you use methamphetamine to aid you in your studies. Initially, you felt like you were on top of the world. You were happy with the results of using meth. As time went on, you needed more and more of it. You couldn't go through a day without it anymore. You went from using it occasionally, then more frequently and finally, multiple times daily. Due to the illicit nature of the substance, you got in trouble with the authorities various times, and you're not even 25 years old.

What started off as a crutch to get you through the pressure turned into what your entire life revolved around. It ended up getting in the way of your college education, which you ended up dropping out of. You were missing important family events. Over one year, you went from an ambitious college student to a troubled college drop-out. You expressed your regret over this. You said that you hadn't expected this of yourself; you always thought you could control your substance intake but very quickly found it to be controlling you. You stated, "It's not that I want to use meth anymore, it's that I must otherwise I go through withdrawals...I can't kick the habit, and I don't see a way out".

*With gratitude,
Dr. Suhaila*

Afterthoughts

The way I see it, the paradigm shift that people with SUD need to understand is that their substance use is no longer a habit; it's a disorder. When patients view what they're going through as a disorder, they can then understand that it can be managed. Often, patients with SUD attribute their disorder to a lack of self-control, so it's a psychiatrist's responsibility to educate them. Referring to Hamad as an addict made him feel like he had a character flaw. Frankly, I dislike using the word "addict", as it has a negative connotation. Using the term "substance use disorder" convinced him of the management plan we discussed together, and he agreed to rehabilitation. The interaction with Hamad taught me something important, which is that taking the

Defining substance use disorder

For substance use to be classified as a disorder, it must be consumed beyond the initial amounts or beyond the period of time intended, with craving, inability to cut down and experiencing withdrawal symptoms in the absence of the substance. Additionally, there's a sense that it takes over a person's life as they spend significant portions of time obtaining and using that substance, to a degree that important life aspects are ignored.[1] Terms related to substance use include tolerance, which refers to a lack of effect if using the same amount of the substance or needing increased amounts of the substance to achieve the desired effect. Another term is dependence, which refers to a psychological or physiological need to continue using the substance, otherwise withdrawal would occur.[2]

What makes SUD difficult to treat is that it leaves a person in a tormenting cycle once they've developed dependence. If they stop, they risk developing anxiety and other withdrawal symptoms. If they continue, they avoid the withdrawal but risk damaging their health. Even if they have a conviction to stop, they feel like their body won't allow them to – as is the case in the next story.

Dear Thomas,

Your wife brought you to the emergency department after you had been referred by your family doctor. Your life circumstances led you to psychological turmoil. You work in a job that you dislike, only to support your wife and children. But you had been deeply unhappy and most likely suffered from depressive episodes. You fixated on your inability to sleep and externalized everything else you were going through, stating that your other issues were purely social.

Five years ago, you started consuming alcohol. You said that you would drink a glass of heavy liquor every night to quell your anxiety and help you fall asleep. Over time, your intake of alcohol increased every night until you weren't only drinking in the nighttime; you were drinking from the time you got home from work until you blacked out or fell asleep. You mentioned that in the past three weeks, it had gotten worse. You stopped going to work and you spent your days intoxicated with alcohol or sleeping. Your wife insisted that you visit your primary doctor, to whom you expressed that you hated the way you were living...and that whenever you drink, you wish to die. Thankfully, your primary doctor referred you to the emergency department so you could be evaluated – which is when I met you.

After interviewing you to gain details regarding your pattern of drinking, I had to assess your risk of self-harm or suicide as this was one of your doctor's main concerns. You responded to me, "I love my children, I love my wife, I just don't love my life". So, I had to frankly ask the question about whether or not you were planning to end your life, and you told me how those thoughts only came about when you were intoxicated with alcohol.

I listened to you describe how you felt helpless about your situation but how badly you wanted help. You stated that you attempted to help yourself independently and suddenly cut off alcohol, but you would be plagued with anxiety and insomnia again. You mentioned that you tried to do this on your own again and again. I watched you tremble as you were showing me your reports; your tremor was severe enough that you dropped everything you tried to hold. You were already going into a withdrawal state, and it was tormenting to see, but I was glad you chose to seek help.

With gratitude,
Dr. Suhaila

Afterthoughts

This story illustrates how something that was once a coping mechanism became an object of dependence, and it's a story that's too common for those with SUD. It starts off as a way to relieve psychological distress and ends up causing more issues as the person is left with psychological and physical distress when they're using as well as when they try to stop; this is why I described it as a vicious cycle. I don't believe anybody voluntarily wants to live their life depending on something to get through the day. I would imagine that Thomas would have ended up on a different path if he sought professional mental health when he was having depressive symptoms, but that doesn't mean he's to blame for developing alcohol use disorder. Sometimes, people don't have the awareness or means to seek help, so they seek help from a bottle or a pill. This is why I felt his story was important to share, in the hopes that anybody in similar circumstances will see a professional for help.

THE BURDEN OF SUBSTANCE USE

Even though I spent quite some time training in the rehabilitation unit, there is a paucity of literature that reflected how much of a burden SUD is in the United Arab Emirates. Overall in the Middle East, a study found that substance use disorder increased by 7.8% from 1990 to 2019.[3] Another study showed that 30 million adults in the region abuse alcohol.[4] Alarmingly, a study in Oman found that 20.7% of people in high school abuse substances.[5] There are devastating consequences for those who start to use substances at such a young age when their brains are still growing and their personalities are yet to be formed – as you'll read in the next story.

Dear Maha,

You walked into the meeting room; your hair was parted down the middle and worn in two neatly done French braids. As you sat down to talk to your doctors, I noticed you smelled of fresh soap. You'd just showered and maintained a decent level of hygiene – which is usually unlikely for somebody who is hospitalized in a psychiatric department.

When I tried to talk to you, you said, "Could you stop talking? I'm trying to read your mind" – that made me chuckle. You were quite the character; your presence always filled the room with some sort of child-like energy. You were polarizing, people either felt for you or felt defensive around you. You deferred every question by talking about mind-reading, your spiritual connection to people and sometimes making extremely racist comments. You interrupted your own speech and made observations. At some point you looked at me at random and said, "You're wearing blue, that's my favorite color."

Even though you were well into your twenties, you spoke like a child. You had bizarre delusions that were probably related to your drug use beginning at a very young age. Normally, a patient like you who admits to polysubstance abuse would be admitted to a rehabilitation center, but you were going through a psychotic episode despite cessation of substance use.

Your story is heartbreaking. At a young age, you found out that your brother was abusing substances, so he coerced you to try them in order to make sure you wouldn't tell your parents on him. From then on, he used you to buy his drugs and exposed you to a world that no adolescent should be subjected to.

Diagnoses are usually difficult to make when there's concomitant substance use, but yours was particularly difficult as you'd been using since adolescence and we had no way of knowing what came first – the symptoms or the substance use.

Your diagnosis was unclear, and your demeanor was always changing. It's unlike someone in a psychotic episode to keep up with self-care or hygiene, yet you did. Your actions were inconsistent with psychosis or mania, but your speech reflected an abnormal thought process. Your management was complicated, as it seemed your mind and personality would always be altered due to a long history of using substances.

You were entertaining to some people and infuriating to other people; I believe that was due to the inconsistency of your behavior. I didn't find myself getting frustrated at your behavior – how could I when I know what you went through? Sadly, some people will write you off as a "drug addict", but I look past that and to me, you will always be the young woman who loves braids and the color blue.

With gratitude,
Dr. Suhaila

Afterthoughts

Maha was a reminder of how complexly our minds work. I wondered, would she have grown up with a childlike personality if it weren't for using substances? What kind of person would she be if her brain chemistry wasn't altered at such a young age? It was clear that she had a mental disorder. At times, she showed symptoms of psychosis. At other times, she showed symptoms of mania with psychosis. But would she have had a mental disorder at all if her brother had kept her out of that part of his life? Nevertheless, her story is a reminder that empathy plays a role in treating those with a history of substance use.

Takeaways

To understand dependence, one should know that it could be a disorder when it takes over the most important aspects of a person's life.

When I was in medical college, I was presenting a case report to my supervisor. In one part of it I said, "The patient is asthmatic, he is also a smoker", and he alerted me to the word I used. "We don't attribute traits to patients; next time say that the patient suffers from asthma and the patient smokes, but don't call him an asthmatic and a smoker", he said.

Likewise, I urge you not to judge or label those with SUD. Doing that reduces what they are to a habit or a disorder. Sometimes, it might not be insulting (like saying "asthmatic") – but many times, it adds a hint of judgement, as though everything a person does is irrelevant to who they are, implying that all they are is their disorder. I learned that using words this way can subconsciously cause bias, almost like saying "this person consumed substances voluntarily, so it's their fault for being an addict". Thinking this way is extremely narrow-minded and may affect the way doctors treat their patients. And it's another reason I dislike the word "addict" – it alienates those people who are suffering.

> *"People use drugs, legal and illegal, because their lives are intolerably painful or dull. They hate their work and find no rest in their leisure."*
>
> —Wendell Berry

References

1. Harrison, P., Cowen, P., Burns, T., & Fazel, M. (2017). The misuse of alcohol and drugs. In *Shorter Oxford Textbook of Psychiatry* (7th ed., pp. 563–565). https://doi.org/10.1093/med/9780198747437.001.0001
2. Ganti, L., Kaufman, M. S., & Blitzstein, S. (2016). *First aid for the psychiatry clerkship* (4th ed., pp. 80–81). McGraw-Hill Education/Medical.
3. Nagi, Y., Al-Ajlouni, Y. A., Ta'ani, A., Bak, M., Makarem, N., & Haidar, A. The Burden of Mental Disorders and Substance Abuse in the Middle East and North Africa (MENA) Region: Findings from the Global Burden of Disease Study. *Available at SSRN 4721668*.
4. Rostam-Abadi, Y., Gholami, J., Shadloo, B., Mohammad Aghaei, A., Mardaneh Jobehdar, M., Ardeshir, M., ... & Rahimi-Movaghar, A. (2024). Alcohol use, alcohol use disorder and heavy episodic drinking in the Eastern Mediterranean region: A systematic review. *Addiction*, *119*(6), 984–997.
5. AS, H. A. A., & Shaikh, J. (2018). Prevalence of substance abuse among the school students in Al-Dhahirah governorate, Sultanate of Oman. *Madridge J Nurs*, *3*(1), 118–123.

Chapter 11

SUICIDE

THE LAST LETTER

Survival is a basic instinct in humanity. As such, one might wonder what is it that leads people to go against that instinct and make the choice to take their own lives? The answer to that is nuanced, and suicide has been described as "an existential paradox".[1] Theories regarding suicide are studied in the fields of psychiatry, abnormal psychology, sociology, and anthropology.

How do we describe suicide?

Understanding suicide and suicidal behavior are imperative due to the potentially lethal consequences. In the field of mental health, we describe suicidality in several different ways. There are passive suicidal ideations, which is when a person wishes to die but does nothing to fulfill that wish. Suicidal ideations could be active; in this case, the person has a death wish, the intention to die and an organized plan – they might even have made preparations and obtained the means required to end their life. Many people use the term "commit" suicide – which suggests that suicide is a crime. As for me, I like to stick to clearer terminology. When suicide fails, I call it a suicide attempt. When a person dies by suicide, I call it a completed suicide.

Myths about suicide

Many people have misconceptions about suicide. Below is a table showing some of the common myths about suicide and the reasons people tend to believe them: [2,3,4]

Myth	Explanation
People who talk about suicide rarely attempt suicide	Trivializing suicide in this way protects people from feeling guilty for ignoring the suicidal person's cry for help or warning signs. It eliminates the responsibility to respond or to have provided support earlier
Suicide happens without warning	
People who are suicidal don't really have the desire or intention to die	
People who attempt suicide do it to gain attention	
All people who are suicidal are diagnosed with a depressive disorder or other mental disorder	This is a denial strategy that people tend to believe in order to excuse suicide and assuage their need to find a reason for it
Suicide is caused by adverse life circumstances	
People who attempt suicide are cowardly or weak	
Suicide is related to environmental causes like the weather or phases of the moon	People attribute high suicide rates in Scandinavian countries to the weather
Asking someone about their suicidal tendencies leads them to an attempt	This is also a denial strategy, since people are uncomfortable with the conversation of suicide or believing it's taboo to speak of

The last point is particularly important, as I've encountered many colleagues or patients' family members who hold the opinion that a psychiatrist shouldn't ask about suicidal ideations. Their rationale is that if we talk about suicide, we give the patient the idea to attempt it. However, there's no evidence to support this.

I can't stress enough how important it is to conduct a suicide risk assessment in healthcare. This includes asking if the ideas are passive death wishes, or active ideations to end one's life with an intention to die (including having an organized plan, making preparations, and obtaining the means for suicide). Doing so could save a life.

THEORIES ABOUT SUICIDE

You might hear people saying that those who attempt suicide don't want to end their existence, but they instead attempt it as an alternative to mental distress. While this is true in many scenarios, suicidality is more complex. In this section, I will provide a brief summary of Durkheim's types of suicide as well as other theories of suicide such as the interpersonal theory, the integrated motivational-volitional model, the three-step theory, and the fluid vulnerability theory.

Emile Durkheim was a French sociologist who established a theory positing four types of suicide: egoistic, altruistic, anomic and fatalistic. *Egoistic suicide* is reflected by a sense of disintegration within a community, resulting from a prolonged feeling of not sufficiently belonging to a social group. People falling into this category don't receive guidance or social support, leading to feelings of meaninglessness and depression. *Altruistic suicide* refers to being integrated within a society, yet viewing one's own needs as unimportant compared to society's needs as a whole. An example of this is if a soldier were to put themselves in harm's way for the good of society. *Anomic suicide* occurs when one lacks social direction and goes through moral confusion. In this case, people attempt suicide as they're in a constant state of disappointment, usually when faced with new expectations. *Fatalistic suicide* occurs when one feels oppressed by strict societal norms. An example of this would be a person whose future is always hampered as a result of repressive discipline. [5]

The interpersonal theory of suicide poses that the concurrent presence of two interpersonal constructs leads to the most dangerous form of suicidal desire. The first construct is termed "thwarted belongingness", which refers to the unmet need to belong and a lack of social connectedness. The second construct is known as "perceived burdensomeness", where an individual believes themselves to be a burden to their loved ones for reasons like family conflict, unemployment or chronic illness. The interpersonal theory highlights that for a potential completed suicide, an individual needs to have suicidal desire and a capacity to act on that desire.[6,7]

The integrated motivational volitional model is somewhat similar to the interpersonal theory. There's the motivational phase, which refers to developing the intention to attempt suicide; and the volitional phase, which has to do with going through with the intention. The motivational phase can develop when one feels entrapped due to negative life circumstances, results in feelings of defeat combined with poor coping skills. The volitional phase has to do with increased capability to attempt suicide, impulsivity and having access to lethal means.[8]

The three-step theory is the one most recently posed to explain how suicidal thoughts progress to suicidal behavior, and it draws from previously explained theories. The first step is forming suicidal ideations in response to the combination of physical or psychological pain and feelings of hopelessness. This implies that when an individual is unable to cope with an aversive life, living can feel like punishment so their inability to imagine a better future makes suicide a more viable option to them. The second step describes how suicidal ideation escalates when feelings of disconnectedness arise. When one's pain precludes them from satisfactory connectedness, suicidal ideations increase and are no longer merely passive death wishes. The third step describes how an individual's strong suicidal ideations are amplified when they have the capacity to go forward with an attempt. This is likely to occur if the individual has a high threshold for pain, lacks fear of death, and has knowledge about and access to lethal means. [9]

The fluid vulnerability theory overlaps with the aforementioned theories but focuses on the suicidal belief system, which takes into account cognitive inflexibility and deficits in emotional regulation.

Unlike other theories, this one focuses on the process of suicide risk over time. It's based on four assumptions. First is that suicide risk is dynamic and based on environmental or individual factors. Second is that suicide risk has some stable factors that are static and unchanging with time. Third is that suicidal behavior results when the dynamic and stable properties intersect. Fourth is that suicidal risk can be mitigated if the appropriate issues can be resolved. [10]

It's paramount to take into consideration the compounded nature of suicide, since understanding these theories can help us empathize with those who are suicidal and assist in developing interventions for suicide prevention.

Risk factors for completed suicide

A clinical assessment tool was developed to determine risk factors for completed suicide. The tool includes the following 10 aspects: male gender, age below 19 or above 45, having a depressive disorder, having a chronic illness, having a previous suicide attempt, being intoxicated with alcohol or other substances, loss of rational thinking, lack of social support, lack of a spouse, and having an organized suicidal plan.[11] The more factors one has, the greater their risk for suicide completion.

The last letter in this book is to show you how loneliness and despair can lead to suicide.

Dear Fahad,

You denied that you attempted to take your own life when I came to see you, even though I was called to assess you after the emergency physicians tended to the injuries you sustained due to a suicide attempt. I suspect that your denial came from a desire not to be hospitalized. However, knowing that previous suicide attempts put you at risk for another completed attempt. I couldn't let you leave the hospital.

"Why do you care? You're probably going to leave the room, listen to your pop music and forget all about me". This struck a nerve; I don't forget my patients – and I am a fan of metal music, not pop music. I wondered if you had negative experiences

with psychiatrists, so you did not want to speak to me. I thought you might assume that I was there to ask you a few questions so that I had information to report to my supervisor and then leave you to the care of others. I decided to attempt to reframe your view of psychiatrists. I put my clipboard down, grabbed a chair, and sat across from your hospital bed.

I decided I was going to use the cues from your speech to try to connect with you. Instead of jumping into a suicide risk assessment, I asked, "What's your favorite kind of music?". So you told me about how you grew up listening to rap music like your brother. I asked who your favorite rapper was, and you were surprised when I recognized him. You then told me about how rap music resonates with the kind of life you've been living. You mentioned getting involved with illicit substances – and I thought "This is my way in". I started asking about your mood, your substance use, and before I could touch on the subject of suicide...you called my bluff. "I thought we were just having a chat, now you're acting like a typical psychiatrist". I usually succeed in getting patients to talk about themselves if I find one interest that we can bond over, but it didn't work with you. You were witty, and you could recognize that I was still trying to conduct a psychiatric assessment; that prompted me to change the subject again.

I asked what you do for a living, you said that you hadn't finished high school and you didn't think you needed to – after all, you were going to become a rapper. Then I asked about how you became interested in this genre of music, and why you felt like it relates to your life. You started talking about your childhood and then you expressed feelings of guilt – but you wouldn't specify what made you feel that way. You avoided the question and said, "I've done horrible things that I don't want to talk about". I wondered if you had an exaggerated sense of guilt due to depression, or if you've taken part in actions that truly consumed you with guilt. At this point, I wondered if you were trying to confuse me so that I wouldn't be able to come up with a reason to keep you in the hospital. The impression I got is that you had a depressive disorder, substance use disorder – or both.

Your emergency physician hadn't finished your medical work-up at that time. I was told you would not provide a sample to see if you'd been intoxicated. When I asked you about it, you said that you didn't see the point and that you hadn't had anything to eat or drink to be able to give a sample anyways.

I requested from the nurse responsible for your care to bring you a meal and plenty of water. I had a hunch that the reason you were speaking a lot about random subjects is due to substance intoxication, but you were well-versed and capable of holding a conversation so well that I couldn't say for sure.

Usually, psychiatrists get 20 minutes with a patient in the psychiatry department to determine what their management plan would be. But with you, the conversation went on much longer. This was due to how many questions you refused to answer and how you deferred questions back to me – as though you were trying to get to know me. Eventually, I had to leave to care for other patients. I told you that your reluctance to answer my questions gave me more of a reason to keep you in the hospital. You responded, "Whatever, you're going to forget about me anyway". So I looked at you and said, "Don't worry, even if you think I can't provide you with the care your need, I will think of you when I listen to your favorite rapper." You chuckled, as if you didn't believe me...but I was alright with it, because I knew that to be true.

With gratitude,
Dr. Suhaila

Afterthoughts

Eventually, it turned out that I was right when I suspected that Fahad was intoxicated. Hours after I had seen him, I got a phone call that his toxicology results were out and positive for a certain substance. It made me wonder if his suicide attempt was due to being intoxicated. It made me wonder if the length of our conversation was due to him being under the influence. He was admitted to the hospital, but not under the team I was working in at that point. I had so many questions in my head about him, including what pushed him to attempt taking his life, how he became dependent on substances, and what would happen to him after he's treated and discharged from the hospital.

The more I thought about it, the more I became alert to Fahad's feelings of loneliness, isolation, and need for connectedness – that's why he attempted to speak with me as a friend rather than answering my questions as a doctor.

I got a phone call from his treating team over the next few days, asking me to re-assess him as he wouldn't speak to anyone about his mental state and requested to see me. When I finally caught a break and went to the toxicology department to see him, they told me he was gone but he left a letter for me. When I opened it, I found that he had written a song about me, and he titled it "Hope". I already knew I wasn't going to forget him, but now I have a reminder that hangs on my wall.

TAKEAWAYS

Thinking about suicide makes me think of the heaviness of being human, and how it becomes too much for a person to the point of wanting to end it. I encounter many people who don't think that suicide happens where they live. My career has enlightened me to how common it actually is. As a trainee physician, I worked 12–16 hours once or twice a week and during those shifts, I was responsible for assessing those who show up in the emergency department after suicide attempts. And I can tell you with conviction that there was nary a shift without a consultation for a suicide attempt. These consultations always weigh heavy; it's only human to feel sad when you meet people who want to die. What makes me even sadder is that I get to consult for the attempted suicides, but there are completed suicides that I never got the chance to help as there are more than 700,000 people who die by suicide per year.

> *"I believe that no man ever threw away life while it was worth keeping."*
>
> —DAVID HUME

I hope we as a society work together to help those suffering with suicidality realize their lives' worth.

REFERENCES

1. Neuringer, C. (1988). The meaning behind popular myths about suicide. *OMEGA - Journal of Death and Dying, 18*(2), 155–162. doi:10.2190/rghw-w8jt-8j6v-lqaj
2. Hubbard, R. W., & McIntosh, J. L. (1992). Integrating suicidology into abnormal psychology classes: the revised facts on suicide quiz. *Teaching of Psychology, 19*(3), 163–166. doi:10.1207/s15328023top1903

3. Segal, D. L. (2001). Levels of knowledge about suicide facts and myths among younger and older adults. *Clinical Gerontologist, 22*(2), 71–80.
4. Neuringer, C. (1988). The meaning behind popular myths about suicide. *OMEGA - Journal of Death and Dying, 18*(2), 155–162. doi:10.2190/rghw-w8jt-8j6v-lqaj
5. Durkheim, E. (2005). *Suicide: A study in sociology.* Routledge.
6. Van Orden, K. A., Witte, T. K., Cukrowicz, K. C., Braithwaite, S. R., Selby, E. A., & Joiner, T. E., Jr (2010). The interpersonal theory of suicide. *Psychological Review, 117*(2), 575–600. https://doi.org/10.1037/a0018697
7. Klonsky, E. D., Saffer, B. Y., & Bryan, C. J. (2018). Ideation-to-action theories of suicide: a conceptual and empirical update. *Current Opinion in Psychology, 22*, 38–43.
8. Ibid.
9. Ibid.
10. Ibid.
11. Patterson, W. M., Dohn, H. H., Bird, J., & Patterson, G. A. (1983). Evaluation of suicidal patients: The SAD PERSONS scale. *Psychosomatics, 24*(4), 343–349. doi:10.1016/s0033-3182(83)73213-5

Chapter 12

Mental Disorders in the Healthcare Field

"MEDICE, CURA TE IPSUM"

Are Psychiatrists Crazy?

Often, we hear people saying that psychiatrists end up with mental disorders because our jobs revolve around patients with mental disorders.

On the other hand, there are those who think psychiatrists should be able to avoid mental disorders *because* we learn how to treat them. Whichever rationale you lean towards, the fact of the matter is no medical specialty is entirely immune to developing mental disorders as statistics show.

I'm certain you've heard of the common saying that doctors make the worst patients. This may stem from a denial that we can have a disorder, mental or physical. I often tell people around me that I dislike going to doctors' appointments because it makes me feel like I'm going back to my place of work – which is not someplace I want to be if I spend 8–16 hours a day there already.

Illness is a State of Vulnerability

Many healthcare workers prefer not to display vulnerability. After all, our job is to treat those with illness, so it's hard to admit when *we* are the ones who need treatment.

Mental Disorders in the Healthcare Field

Being a healthcare worker involves multiple risk factors for developing mental disorders:

- Long working hours
- Unpredictable shift work
- Working during weekends or holidays
- Constantly being surrounded by illness and death.

These risk factors subject us to burnout, mental distress, and mental disorders.

A study found that doctors in specialty training are particularly prone to mental distress, as the nature of their job includes sleep deprivation, transitioning roles, and frequent relocation, which could result in a lack of adequate support as well as feelings of isolation.[1]

Personal attributes like an amplified sense of duty and responsibility, as well as the pressure of attempting perfectionism with an exaggerated attention to detail, contribute to stress and depression in healthcare workers.[2]

STATISTICALLY SPEAKING

It was difficult to find statistics regarding the mental wellbeing of healthcare professionals in the UAE prior to the COVID-19 pandemic. However, during and after the pandemic, research was more robust. Studies found that PTSD was the most common mental health impact of the pandemic.[3,4]

Other findings included healthcare workers experiencing contamination anxiety at a high level, moderate to severe sleep disturbances, and substance use.[5] Another study that took place in Dubai found that healthcare workers experienced mental fatigue and social discrimination more than the public.[6] Anxiety and depression were reported at significant levels in additional studies.[7] Studies that have been conducted globally found similar results.[8]

Apart from the healthcare impact of the pandemic, there are general statistics regarding mental disorders within the healthcare sector well worth noting. Statistics from the American Medical Association showed that the specialties reporting the highest rates of mild to severe depressive symptoms are as follows: [9]

1. Urology: 38.5%
2. Emergency medicine: 38.3%
3. Family medicine: 35.8%
4. Obstetrics and gynecology: 33.6%
5. General internal medicine: 33.3%
6. Physical medicine and rehabilitation: 32.7%
7. Radiology: 32%
8. Pediatric subspecialty: 31.9%
9. Psychiatry: 31.8%
10. Dermatology: 31.6%.

In 2021, an op-ed was published about two trainee doctors who took their own lives in New York City.[10] Though it's known that all healthcare workers are prone to mental disorders, these completed suicides prompted the public to pay more attention to the issue.

That same year, the Canadian Medical Association surveyed more than 4,000 doctors and medical students and found that 48% suffered from depressive symptoms and around 15% experienced moderate to severe anxiety. Another study revealed that 21.7% of healthcare workers experienced thoughts of suicide with up to 3.5% attempting suicide. [11]

Suicide evaluation in healthcare workers became a topic of research. A meta-analysis showed that the specialties at high risk for suicide were anesthesiologists, psychiatrists, family medicine doctors, and general surgeons. Anesthesiologists' risk factors include easy access to potentially lethal medications, combined with their high workload and prevalence of burnout. Psychiatrists are prone to attempting suicide due to witnessing traumatic experiences unironically, like their known patients completing suicide. Family medicine doctors are at risk as they experience moral loneliness, disruption of work–life balance, and dealing with high levels of patients' expectations. Surgeons sometimes have to deal with life-and-death emergencies with very limited time, which is a pressure great enough to pose as a risk factor. All these factors in different specialties amount to a higher risk of suicide. [12] This information prompts interventions for healthcare workers in order to reduce the risk of mental disorders and suicide.

"Medice, cura te ipsum" translates to "physician, heal thyself", but we would be remiss to leave healthcare workers to care for themselves. Those who take care of others deserve to be taken care of as well.

Giving a Voice to Struggling Healthcare Workers

For a more personal take on mental disorders in the healthcare sector, I interviewed a doctor who lives with a mental disorder and continues to work. The guest doctor agreed to this interview but prefers to stay anonymous.

Dr. Suhaila: *Hello Doctor, thank you for agreeing to speak with me. How are you feeling today?*
Guest Doctor: *I'm feeling well.*

Dr. Suhaila: *Since I know you're short on time, let's get right into it. My first question is, would you mind telling me when you were diagnosed with a mental disorder?*
Guest Doctor: *I was diagnosed when I was in medical college.*

Dr. Suhaila: *Can you tell me about the symptoms that led to your diagnosis?*
Guest Doctor: *I felt depressed and withdrawn, I was not sleeping well, I had poor concentration and felt fatigued to the point that it affected academic performance.*

Dr. Suhaila: *How did the symptoms you were experiencing affect your day-to-day studies?*
Guest Doctor: *One of my symptoms was that I lost the will to do things, I lost the will to study. Combined with low energy, I reached to a point of sitting for exams without studying.*

Dr. Suhaila: *How does the diagnosis of a mental disorder affect your day-to-day work?*
Guest Doctor: *I have prolonged absences due to relapses. Certain medications I take affect my sleep, and that becomes an issue when I am posted for night shifts as I am forced to skip nighttime doses of my medication.*

Dr. Suhaila: *Does taking medications affect your work as a doctor?*
Guest Doctor: *It does not. However, when my medications need adjustments; that requires me to take time off – which does affect how supervisors and colleagues perceive my performance. But taking medications does not affect how I think, perform, or go about my usual duties as a doctor.*

Dr. Suhaila: *Do you doubt your abilities as a doctor because you have a mental disorder?*
Guest Doctor: *Sometimes, from time to time when I am going through a relapse.*

Dr. Suhaila: *How do you deal with self-doubt?*
Guest Doctor: *I reach out to friends who reframe my thoughts and remind me of how well I am actually performing instead of believing the doubts I have about my performance.*

Dr. Suhaila: *Does being a doctor make you more or less likely to seek help?*
Guest Doctor: *It makes me less likely to seek help. Sadly, others might view it as a weakness and view you as less qualified. They might start to doubt your skills or the way you carry out your work. By not seeking help, I might be viewed as a doctor who performs better. Paradoxically, instead of worrying about my own mental health (which will positively affect my work), I would delay taking care of myself and overwork myself to compensate for the perceived deficits that come with having a mental disorder.*

Dr. Suhaila: *Do you believe doctors with a mental disorder shouldn't be in this field?*
Guest Doctor: *Of course not. Empathy is an important aspect of a doctor's attitude and having a mental disorder makes a doctor more understanding of a patient's situation.*

Dr. Suhaila: *Do you believe doctors with a mental disorder are less competent?*

Guest Doctor: *No. It's not just what I believe, it's from experience. I personally know doctors diagnosed with a mental disorder and I've witnessed how competent they are.*

Dr. Suhaila: *Do you disclose your diagnosis with your supervisors or colleagues?*

Guest Doctor: *I prefer not to disclose it. If I was in a situation like a relapse, I would disclose it to my direct supervisor in order to ensure patient safety. However, I would rather not disclose it to my counterparts as I believe it is personal and there is a stigma attached to it.*

Dr. Suhaila: *Do you feel that you would be discriminated against at work if others knew about your diagnosis?*

Guest Doctor: *Yes, I have experienced it first-hand. I had to undergo certain kinds of training in a different way than my counterpart colleagues and at times, I was mandated to take a leave of absence due to my supervisors' opinion that my condition affects how I work.*

Dr. Suhaila: *In what ways do you cope with having a stressful job and mental disorder?*

Guest Doctor: *I manage to cope by having a circle of support, that includes friends, family and professional help.*

Dr. Suhaila: *When going through an acute mental crisis, have you ever engaged in harmful behavior?*
Guest Doctor: *Yes, but I would rather not elaborate.*

Dr. Suhaila: *Who do you turn to for support when you're having an acute mental crisis?*
Guest Doctor: *I would most likely reach out to a friend.*

Dr: Suhaila: *Since the COVID-19 pandemic, has your mental health deteriorated as a result?*
Guest Doctor: *Not really.*

Dr. Suhaila: *Do you believe that the COVID-19 pandemic has negatively affected healthcare providers who were already struggling with mental health issues?*
Guest Doctor: *Yes, it did. Many of them could not return back to their homes and faced social isolation.*

Dr. Suhaila: *What is your advice for anyone diagnosed with a mental disorder and thinking of pursuing the medical field? Or would you advise them not to go into the field?*

Guest Doctor: *My advice is to prioritize themselves and their mental health over everything else, because when they do that, their lives – both personally and professionally – would be better. But if they prioritize studies and work over their wellbeing, they will inevitably deteriorate, and their recovery would be more complicated. I hope they recognize that it's okay if they need to take a break since everybody's career trajectory is different. I wouldn't advise them against going into the field, I would just advise them to take good care of themselves as it will one day be their responsibility to care for others.*

Dr. Suhaila: *Knowing what you know now, what would you go back and tell yourself when you were diagnosed with a mental disorder?*

Guest Doctor: *I would give myself the same advice I mentioned above since I personally experienced de-prioritizing my mental wellbeing, and it did not go well. I would have given attention to my issues as they were arising rather than waiting until I faced a mental health crisis. Not doing so resulted in a longer time for recovery, as well as the severity of the issues over time which affected my day-to-day life.*

Dr. Suhaila: *Any last words?*

Guest Doctor: *I want people to recognize that everything in life is temporary and everything eventually passes. Don't be afraid to ask for help, even if there are consequences to doing so; the priority should be your health and your life.*

Dr. Suhaila: *Thank you for your time and honesty. I wish you well in all your endeavors.*

I believe this doctor's story is an inspiration for everyone who continues to work in healthcare even with a mental disorder; it's someone that I genuinely admire. I'm thankful for this doctor's bravery and willingness to speak openly and honestly about their struggle as well as provide advice based on their own experience.

This doctor found a way to adjust to a work environment that's inherently stressful for anyone, especially for those with a chronic disorder. Through receiving the appropriate treatment and relying on loved ones for support, not only are they a role model for others – they also provide hope.

TAKEAWAYS

Despite challenges, healthcare continues to be a rewarding job. From my own personal experience, I've found that being a healthcare worker in the United Arab Emirates is a special experience given that our country is open to many cultures. Throughout my college years and career, I practiced psychiatry in Dubai and Abu Dhabi.

As a student, I also did a short rotation in Dublin, Ireland where most of my patients were Irish. I happened to meet an Amish Mennonite patient, who was the one different patient during my experience. I learned a lot from one significantly different patient. I remember one of my supervisors telling me that it's important to speak your patient's language. In the literal sense that's true, but she had meant it metaphorically in that I needed to explain their illness to them in a way that they can accept. That was one difficult interaction in Ireland, but it's almost a daily occurrence in the UAE.

Specializing in psychiatry in the UAE is an experience that exposes you to how people from different backgrounds and socioeconomic statuses live.

And that challenge is eye-opening and provides you with the opportunity to understand how to help a variety of people. The beauty of what we do is that it expands our worldview.

And finally, I wouldn't want to be anything other than a psychiatrist.

> *"Psychiatry is like no other specialty; it transcends a mere medicine of the body to touch upon fundamental questions about our identity, purpose and potential."*[13]
>
> —Jeffrey A. Lieberman

References

1. Goldman, M. L., Shah, R. N., & Bernstein, C. A. (2015). Depression and suicide among physician trainees. *JAMA Psychiatry, 72*(5), 411. doi:10.1001/jamapsychiatry.2014.3050
2. Dutheil, F., Aubert, C., Pereira, B., Dambrun, M., Moustafa, F., Mermillod, M., et al. (2019). Suicide among physicians and healthcare workers: A systematic review and

meta-analysis. *PLoS ONE*, *14*(12): e0226361. https://doi.org/10.1371/journal.pone.0226361

3. Aljawarneh, Y.M., Ghader, N., Al-Bashaireh, A.M., Dalky, H.F., Al-Omari, H., Alkouri, O., Sanad, S.R., Mheiri, N.A., Gopakumar, A., AlShaya, S., et al. (2024). Exploring risk perception, mental health, mental fatigue, stigma, and the quality of life among UAE healthcare workers during the COVID-19 pandemic: a national multicentric cross-sectional study. *International Journal of Environmental Research and Public Health*, *21*(9): 1124. https://doi.org/10.3390/ijerph21091124

4. Al Dhaheri, A. S., Bataineh, M. F., Mohamad, M. N., Ajab, A., Al Marzouqi, A., Jarrar, A. H., Habib-Mourad, C., Abu Jamous, D. O., Ali, H. I., Al Sabbah, H., Hasan, H., Stojanovska, L., Hashim, M., Abd Elhameed, O. A., Shaker Obaid, R. R., ElFeky, S., Saleh, S. T., Osaili, T. M., & Cheikh Ismail, L. (2021). Impact of COVID-19 on mental health and quality of life: Is there any effect? A cross-sectional study of the MENA region. *PloS One*, *16*(3), e0249107. https://doi.org/10.1371/journal.pone.0249107

5. Aljawarneh, Y.M., Ghader, N., Al-Bashaireh, A.M., Dalky, H.F., Al-Omari, H., Alkouri,

O., Sanad, S.R., Mheiri, N.A., Gopakumar, A., AlShaya, S., et al. (2024). Exploring risk perception, mental health, mental fatigue, stigma, and the quality of life among UAE healthcare workers during the COVID-19 pandemic: a national multicentric cross-sectional study. *International Journal of Environmental Research and Public Health*, *21*(9):1124. https://doi.org/10.3390/ijerph21091124

6. Saddik, B.; Elbarazi, I.; Temsah, M.H.; Saheb Sharif-Askari, F.; Kheder, W.; Hussein, A.; Najim, H.; Bendardaf, R.; Hamid, Q.; Halwani, R. (2021). Psychological distress and anxiety levels among health care workers at the height of the COVID-19 pandemic in the United Arab Emirates. *Int. J. Public Health*, *66*, 1604369.

7. Cheikh Ismail, L., Mohamad, M. N., Bataineh, M. F., Ajab, A., Al-Marzouqi, A. M., Jarrar, A. H., Abu Jamous, D. O., Ali, H. I., Al Sabbah, H., Hasan, H., Stojanovska, L., Hashim, M., Shaker Obaid, R. R., Saleh, S. T., Osaili, T. M., & Al Dhaheri, A. S. (2021). Impact of the Coronavirus pandemic (COVID-19) lockdown on mental health and well-being in the United Arab Emirates. *Frontiers in*

Psychiatry, *12*, 633230. https://doi.org/10.3389/fpsyt.2021.633230

8. Marvaldi, M., Mallet, J., Dubertret, C., Moro, M. R., & Guessoum, S. B. (2021). Anxiety, depression, trauma-related, and sleep disorders among healthcare workers during the COVID-19 pandemic: A systematic review and meta-analysis. *Neuroscience and Biobehavioral Reviews*, *126*, 252–264. https://doi.org/10.1016/j.neubiorev.2021.03.024

9. AMA (2024). Top 10 physician specialties with the highest rates of depression. *American Medical Association*. https://www.ama-assn.org/practice-management/physician-health/top-10-physician-specialties-highest-rates-depression

10. Aponte, C. I. (2021). Lincoln hospital doctor trainees say harsh culture took toll before three died. *The City* [Preprint]. Available at: https://www.thecity.nyc/2021/7/29/22601128/bronx-lincoln-hospital-doctor-trainees-toxic-culture-three-deaths

11. García-Iglesias, J. J., Gómez-Salgado, J., Fernández-Carrasco, F. J., Rodríguez-Díaz, L., Vázquez-Lara, J. M., Prieto-Callejero, B., & Allande-Cussó, R. (2022). Suicidal ideation and suicide attempts in healthcare professionals

during the COVID-19 pandemic: A systematic review. *Frontiers in Public Health*, *10*, 1043216. https://doi.org/10.3389/fpubh.2022.1043216

12. Dutheil, F., Aubert, C., Pereira, B., Dambrun, M., Moustafa, F., Mermillod, M., et al. (2019). Suicide among physicians and health-care workers: A systematic review and meta-analysis. *PLoS ONE*, 14*(12)*: e0226361. https://doi.org/10.1371/journal. pone.0226361

13. Lieberman, J. A. (2016). *Shrinks: The untold story of psychiatry.* Back Bay Books.

CONCLUSION

I hope that reading the stories shared humanizes those living with a mental disorder, as this book is meant to provide a basic understanding of different mental disorders. In addition, I set out to dispel some of the misconceptions revolving around certain subjects.

One of the aims of this book is for those struggling to know that there are safe spaces to open up about their strife. Family, friends, and healthcare professionals could all be positive protective factors. Additionally, this book is for those who support anyone who might be struggling to understand and empathize with their situation. And lastly, it's for healthcare providers who have a curiosity about psychiatry.

Support could take different forms. If you know somebody who's struggling, I suggest that you don't directly ask them, "How can I help?". Doing so puts pressure on them to figure things out when they already feel lost.

Instead, do small things for them without pushing them. These small acts could be sending a message or email to let them know you're thinking of them without expecting a response. (That defeats the purpose, and it serves your own interest.) Other small acts could be to ask if they need help doing chores or tasks, if they need a ride someplace, if they need someone to go with them to a doctor's appointment, or if they'd simply like some food and company. And don't be offended if they're resistant – people living with mental disorders often feel like a burden already, and might sometimes refuse help because they don't want to feel like *more* of a burden. It's unwise to add to the guilt they may be feeling.

Another goal of writing this book was to reduce skepticism when it comes to topics that might seem taboo to speak of, so as to start the conversation and keep it going. When we don't talk about mental wellbeing, people are less likely to seek

Conclusion

help when they need it most. Failing to engage in conversations regarding mental disorders limits our understanding of them, which inevitably leads to poor health outcomes. Trivializing mental disorders or refusing to acknowledge their reality is harmful. As such, society as a whole stands to benefit from learning more about mental wellbeing.

People need people; we are not a species that thrives from being lone wolves. We thrive and grow when connecting with others. When we are mentally well, it enables us to better tackle the challenges of life that inevitably occur – whether they're personal or professional. And we're more likely to be mentally well if we can safely rely on others.

I would like to reiterate what I began this book mentioning, which is that there's no health without mental health.

May this book act as a seed that grows to provide hope.

ACKNOWLEDGEMENTS

My career was made possible by the support I received from my family and friends.

My parents, who put me through medical college, deserve much acknowledgement. Mr. Abdulla Hussein AlShaali and Mrs. Maryam Rashed AlShaali – if it wasn't for my education and career, I wouldn't have been able to write this book.

All my siblings deserve an acknowledgement for their faith in me – Mr. Sultan, Ms. Fatima, Mr. Rashid, Mrs. Amani, Ms. Aisha, and Mr. Hussein.

My chosen family has gotten me through some of my darkest days; you know who you are. Thank you.

AUTHOR BIO

Suhaila is a book lover, music appreciator, art enthusiast, candle collector, dog and cat admirer, the list goes on due to her multitude of interests. When she is not working, she dabbles in baking, learning the piano, fitness, and writing.

Suhaila graduated from medical school in 2018. She completed her training as an intern then as a psychiatry resident in 2023. She is currently a practicing board-certified psychiatry specialist and an MSc candidate.

Suhaila has a dog named Aristotle.

Contact and Connect:
linkedin.com/in/suhaila512

www.ingramcontent.com/pod-product-compliance
Lightning Source LLC
Chambersburg PA
CBHW020530080526
44583CB00013B/800